IMPROVING YOUR FINISHED WINE

"Ah my Beloved, fill the cup that clears
Today of past Regrets and Future Fears."
                    — The Rubaiyat of Omar Khayyam

To "Pussy" and cat lovers everywhere.

IMPROVING YOUR FINISHED WINE

by

JOHN MITCHELL

© The "Amateur Winemaker" Publications Ltd. 1978

ISBN 0 900841 50 8

1st EDITION

First Impression April 1978

Printed in Great Britain by
Standard Press (Andover) Ltd., South St. Andover, Hants

PREFACE

Scientific knowledge is always advancing, and whilst this book is correct at the time of going to press in relation to permitted practices and materials as described in the text, changes may take place in the future.

The desire to improve a wine is to seek better quality. Without this quest, mediocrity soon becomes the norm.

J.R.M.

CONTENTS

9

INTRODUCTION

MAKING wine at home has, during the last ten years, become one of the most popular hobby activities in the United Kingdom. No doubt high taxation has helped to increase popularity amongst some sections of the community, but even accepting this to be the case, a multi-million pound industry is now involved in supplying winemakers with equipment and ingredients.

Expertise shown by winemakers has likewise increased over the last decade, and much good wine is made, perhaps in some small way the result of my earlier book, *Scientific Winemaking —made easy*. However, problems do occur, and it was as a result of dealing with those brought to my attention by my many friends who make wine, that I wrote this book. It is intended to help both the beginner and the experienced winemaker to obtain the best results from the money and time expended in making wine at home.

CHAPTER 1

—ASSESSING THE QUALITY—

IF it is assumed that wine has been made using any of the many thousands of recipes available or using the principles put forward in *Scientific Winemaking—made easy*, the first requirement is to obtain some idea of what "quality" has been obtained.

Quality is one of those words which conjures up different meanings depending upon the circumstances. With wine, the essential areas for quality assessment can be grouped as follows:

1. VISUAL

What the eye sees; that is to say, if the wine is clear or cloudy, white, brown, red or some other colour. If it is polished and very clear or cloudy in appearance.

It is upon the answers to these often unconsciously evaluated points that the first quality judgement of a wine is based.

2. AROMA

The bouquet, aroma or smell of a wine tells a lot about its character and origin. Not all fruits betray themselves in the aroma produced in the finished wine. Gooseberry for instance, can, if properly made, resemble a grape wine in its bouquet. At the other end of the scale, a wine with an aroma resembling nail varnish (amyl acetate) must always be suspected of having been mishandled and allowed to deteriorate. Obviously, aroma therefore plays an important role in quality assessment.

3. TASTE

Tasting a wine should strengthen the opinions already formed by looking and smelling it. At the same time other facets of quality will be revealed. A good balance of acidity with vinosity and sweetness will be more indicative of good quality than an acid taste which suggests the wine would have been better used to top up a car battery!

How then can these quality factors be best assessed?

Tasting requirements

The only equipment required for tasting is a sheet of white paper together with one or more glasses of the tulip-like shape illustrated below in Fig. 1.

FIG. 1.

Also required is a table lamp with a low wattage bulb and the shade removed, a notebook and a pencil. At one time a candle was considered the only light by which to judge wine, but this is really useful only for the assessment of clarity. Smell the glass intended for tasting as a glass cloth used for drying or polishing can impart a quite undesirable aroma to a glass during wiping. For this reason, glasses are often washed, rinsed in cold water and left in an inverted position to drain dry.

Tasting technique

The order in which to examine a wine is clarity, colour, bouquet and, finally, palate. Observations are best noted whilst actually looking, smelling or tasting a wine as the case might be—notes are more accurate when made in this fashion.

When more than one wine is tasted at a session, it is best to taste white before red and dry before sweet, to preserve the sensitivity of the palate.

First write down the type and origin of the wine along with its age. An example might be:

White Gooseberry, made 1976

Before pouring out any wine from a bottle, note if a sediment or deposit exists. If it does, make a note also indicating if it is fine, coarse, or crystalline and if it is coloured. A brown deposit in a white wine would indicate the wine was contaminated with copper, or severe oxidation had taken place, whilst a white or creamy breadcrumb-like deposit is more likely to be yeast which has carried out a secondary fermentation after the wine was bottled. A red wine will often throw a deposit consisting of tannin, colouring and/or protein matter: nevertheless it should be noted as it may give a guide to the "bottle age" of the wine or explain some observation made later. Brown wines can throw a brownish deposit of unstable protein matter, which is due to the inclusion of colouring in the deposit.

Having carried out the preliminary examination, carefully pour (or decant) enough wine to fill the glass, which must be free from taint, about one-third full.

Using the electric light, examine the wine for clarity. All wines should be clear. If any fibres are present, make a note to this effect. They could have come from the filter.

Tip the glass at an angle of 45° over the white paper and examine the "rim" as shown below in Fig. 2.

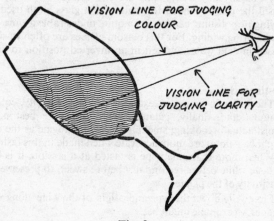

VISION LINE FOR JUDGING COLOUR

VISION LINE FOR JUDGING CLARITY

Fig. 2.

By using the Glossary of Terms, note the colour of the wine. White is meaningless except as a general classification, and can range from water-white to amber when used in connection with wines, therefore something more explicit is required. Explicit notes are also necessary with red, rose and dessert wines—describing the depth of colour takes a little practice and the Glossary explains the meaning of "full", "medium" and "pale".

Nose, bouquet and aroma

A great deal can be told from this assessment. The olfactory senses are able to distinguish the aroma of the ingredients—such as the odour of raspberries in young raspberry wine—as well as the esters apparent in a mature wine—and these characteristics form the bouquet.

Besides assessing the quality of a wine, another important reason for smelling it is for guidance as to whether it should be tasted or not. If a smell like nail varnish, or wine vinegar, cork, rain-water butt or any other offensive smell is apparent, then of course, the wine should not be tasted, or at least not until any other tasting has been done, and then with caution.

If a wine has little or no bouquet, this could be because it is very young or lacking in character and until the tasting is complete, a conclusion cannot be drawn. Young wines have a yeasty or rather aldehydic character which is sharp on the nose whilst wines which have aged to some degree are softer and do not have this sharpness.

An assessment of the depth of bouquet, if a fruity aroma is present and if so, how much, and the general impression of the aroma should be noted.

Palate or taste

Many of the opinions formed from a study of clarity, colour and bouquet are crystallised into a complete assessment by this appraisal.

The things to be looked for are:

1. *Body:* This means the feel of the wine in the mouth, if it is light and rather delicate, or heavy and robust. This is, amongst other things, an indication of the alcohol and extractable solids present. A pronounced taste of alcohol

15

indicates either the wine was more sugar and water than anything else or that, in the case of a fortified dessert wine, the fortification was relatively recent and the wine has not "married" together with the spirit properly.

2. *Acidity:* Some acidity is necessary to provide balance and keeping properties but it should not predominate.

3. *Sweetness or dryness:* This is self-explanatory to a large extent, but what needs to be understood is that astringency— a drying of the roof of the mouth and clinging to the teeth— is not the same as a dry finish due to all the sugar being fermented into alcohol—one is due to tannin and the other to sugar, or lack of it.

4. *Flavour:* The important thing is to record what is tasted in terms that can be understood by someone else. If the flavour is reminiscent of blackcurrant juice, then this is the best way to describe it. Fruitiness is a fleshy texture more than a flavour and shows the fruit origin rather than just a flavouring.

5. *Balance:* When a wine is balanced, all characteristics harmonise, with nothing predominating in an offending manner. The body, alcoholic content, flavour, tannin and acidity combine to form the wine style required. For instance, a sweet wine should not in any way appear dry either in the taste or after taste, otherwise it would be unbalanced.

VISUAL

1. Clarity

Brilliant	That degree of clarity which makes the wine "sparkle" like cut glass.
Clear	Indicates that no deposit is present or haze suspended in the wine, and that filter fibres or any other foreign bodies are absent.
Clot	A clot on the top of the wine indicates very inefficient pectin removal. Small clots in the wine also indicate pectin or unstable protein matter.
Deposit	A sediment formed at the bottom of the bottle.
	Secondary fermentation produces a yeast deposit which is off-white and can be either fine or crumb-like, depending on the yeast.
	Metal contamination produces a deposit or casse the colour of which is usually off-white or grey whilst copper is commonly brown.
Hazy	A fine haze or cloud. This could be the result of poor fining removal, metal contamination or protein deposits.
Homogeneity	Any sign of mixing should be suspected as it suggests poor blending just before bottling.
Silky haze	A silky sheen on the haze. This usually indicates a bacterial infection. Often the bottle has to be swirled to see this effect.

2. Sparkling

A good gas content in the wine. It effervesces well and does not go flat quickly.

3. Colour

The term "Red" is meaningless without qualification as any motor car dealer knows. The same is true in relation to the colour of wines.

(a) Tint

Colourless	Water-white—as in Vodka or Gin.
White	Means very little on its own and should be avoided except to classify broadly.
Pale Straw	A colour like that of a drinking straw.
Straw	The colour of a straw stook as seen on a farm. This is a pleasing pale yellow colour.
Pale Lemon	The colour of clear pure lemon juice, freshly pressed with just the faintest tinge of green present.
Golden	A bright golden hue as seen in sugar syrup. This colour is often associated with sweeter wines.
Brown/Gold	The appearance of a brown tinge in a "white" wine usually means oxidation has set in and the wine is past its best. In a dessert wine it is quite normal or where dried fruit has been used which is rich in caramelised sugar.
Pale Brown	The colour of an amontillado sherry. Quite a good shade for an aperitif.
Mid-Brown	The tint of mild ale. A good shade for a dessert style wine.
Brown	A shade like chop sauce. Not a very good colour except for the heaviest dessert wines.
Rosé	The delicate pink seen in rose petals and should be reserved for describing the light tinge of true rosé wines.
Pink	Self-descriptive but should not have any orange or blue tinges. Often used for pink wines of deeper hue than Rosé.
Orange/Pink	An orange tinted pink. This can be attractive and yet still not be pink or rosé. Sometimes it indicates the blending of white and red wines.
Orange	A pale orange tint usually indicates the blending of wines to produce what is hoped to be a rosé.

18

Ruby	A red colour like that of Port wine.
Red-Brown	The pure red changing to a shade which has a little brown in it. This indicates the wine has some maturity unless a blending of red and brown wine has taken place.
Purple	A blue red colour. Young wines often have this colour.
Mahogany	A rich deep tone of genuine mahogany furniture. When this is noted in what was a *red* wine either the wine has matured very well or has deteriorated through oxidation.
Tawny	A light mahogany shade.

(b) *Depth of Tone* (important for red wines)

Pale	The depth of colour is not very great. For example, a bottle of blackcurrant syrup has great depth of colour, but a teaspoonful of syrup in a glass of water will have the same tint but be pale. Thus a wine could be described as "Pale Red/ Purple".
Medium	The next step up from pale. Most ruby ports or Beaujolais wines could have this description.
Full	The depth of tone encountered in a good elderberry wine or, in the wines of commerce, a Chateau Neuf du Pape. Almost, but not quite, opaque.

4. Aroma (Bouquet) The important thing here is to write what it smells like in terms you and others will understand.

Aroma	Smell
Burnt	Either excessive cooking of ingredients or storage too near a heat source.
Caramelised	This smell is a sign that the wine has either been made from fruit which was over cooked or allowed to overage and become oxidised.
Clean	No off-flavours present.

Corky or Musty	The smell similar to a dry cork which has been in a moist but otherwise empty medicine bottle for some time.
Damp Paper	A smell like that produced when boiling water is poured on to paper pulp. The filter was incompletely washed.
Earthy	A smell akin to damp soil. If Bentonite fining has been done it might mean too high a dose was used.
Fragrant	A perfumed aroma, delicate and flowery.
Fruity	Indicates the aroma is like that of a fruit and is best qualified with a description of which fruit, viz., "Clean and fruity with a banana-like aroma."
Green	A term often used to mean young and immature; it is characterised by an aldehydic aroma and often a yeasty smell.
Peardrops or a Nail Varnish-like smell	A danger sign, often an indication that the wine is turning slightly acetic. A bacterial infection or oxidation defect is immediately suspected.
Rotten Eggs	Wines which have just finished fermenting sometimes have this aroma due to hydrogen sulphide gas produced by the yeasts reducing sulphur bodies dissolved in the wine. This will often gradually disappear with racking and subsequent operations to clarify. However, sometimes it is necessary to take special steps to remove it and these are described in Chapter 3.
Faint, medium, Full	Used to describe the depth of aroma. Faint means little bouquet at all, and so on.
Spirity	Alcoholic aroma can mean that the wine is rather raw and unbalanced or that fortification has taken place.
Stalky	The smell of freshly cut twiggs. Often indicates a young wine.

Sulphury	The smell of a London fog or air near a brickworks. A sign of too much sulphur dioxide.
Sweet	Self-explanatory.
Woody	A smell like a rain water butt which indicates the wine was at some time in a poor wooden cask or was left too long in wood.
Yeasty	A smell like bakers' yeast often present in new young wine which will gradually disappear with racking and ageing.

5. Palate (Taste)

Alcoholic	The pronounced flavour of alcohol indicates very little natural ingredients (sugar and water used too well) or poor fortification.
Acid	A wine must have some acidity to give it zest and prevent it being flat or insipid but it should not predominate so much as to give tartness and overpower all the other characteristics.
Astringent	A drying of the mouth. When due to excess tannin, this is unpleasant. A little tannin in a red wine is, however desirable.
Balanced	A satisfactory combination of alcohol content, acidity, tannin and flavour to give a pleasing taste.
Bitter	A taste sometimes encountered due to wrong fruit handling. Some fruit skins if fermented with the wine will give this taste. See also Metallic.
Body	The feel of the wine in the mouth—its weight due to alcohol and extracted solids present. It can be light, medium or heavy.
Cooked	A caramel-like flavour encountered when the wine ingredients were either cooked or over-pressure cooked, or the temperature of the fermentation was rather high.

21

Coarse	A roughness associated with rather poor wine.
Cloying	Sweet and heavy not offset with the necessary acidity.
Dry	All the sugar fermented out. This does not mean the mouth is dried out, or astringency.
Earthy	Either poorly chosen or incompletely cleansed ingredients or overfining with Bentonite.
Fresh	Pleasant fresh acidity and refreshing to drink.
Fruity	Taste of fruit. If possible an idea of what fruit the taste is reminiscent should be recorded. It does not matter if this was not the fruit used—conveying what was tasted is important.
Flat	Lacking zest. Can be due to low acidity, low alcohol or over-ageing.
Green	Young and rather immature. Indicates a lack of "marrying" together which will come with age.
Hard	Severe taste due to excess of tannin.
Harsh	Alcohol predominates in the taste over everything else.
Insipid	A wine lacking character, flat and without the necessary acidity.
Mellow	Smoothness due to the glycerol of the wine and age.
Metallic	A bitter clinging taste due to contamination of the wine with probably iron (less often from copper).
Medium Dry	A basically dry wine with just a trace of sweetness.
Medium Sweet	A wine which is sweet but not in a pronounced manner.
Mousey	A most unpleasant and often bitter taste and after-taste, accompanied by the smell of mice can indicate a bacterial infection. A haze should be carefully

	looked for in an attempt to support this.
Prickle	A tickle on the tongue due to dissolved carbon dioxide in the wine. In what is supposed to be a still wine, this indicates a secondary or malolactic fermentation has taken place whilst the wine was in bottle.
Robust	A term used for red wines to mean balanced, full-bodied, and full-flavoured with a fruity texture.
Round	All the characteristics of the wine integrated to form a mellow, smooth quality.
Rich	A wine having qualities full and luscious to the palate and senses.
Smooth	No obvious excess of acidity or tannin—a well-balanced and mature wine.
Soft	Bland, astringency absent and agreeable to the palate.
Sweet	Residual sugar in the wine.
Tannin	Tannin is evidenced by a drying of the mouth and a "grip" on the teeth. It can mean a very young wine is being tasted which will in the course of ageing precipitate much of the excess—or a poorly made wine with too much tannin in the fruit, or excessive addition of tannin.
Tart	A wine giving the impression of unripe fruit or excess acidity.
Woody	A twiggy taste which can be due to the wine being stored in a cask with a new immatured stave.
Unbalanced	A wine with a lack or excess of acid, fruit, tannin or body and where the constituents do not harmonise and balance each other to form the wine style desired.

Having objectively assessed the wine in terms of appearance, aroma, and palate, it is possible to draw conclusions about what action is necessary to improve the wine. The following chapters are designed to assist in carrying out the corrective procedures which can be employed to make improvements.

CHAPTER 2

—IMPROVING THE APPEARANCE—

THE first chapter described how a critical examination of a wine can be made. On the basis of the information obtained, various operations can be performed to improve the quality of the wine. This chapter deals with clarity and colour.

CLARITY
If a wine has a haze or deposit the first thing to establish is the cause, since upon this information will rest the decision of how best to remove it.

Hazes
Broadly speaking hazes or deposits are due to either the activity of micro-organisms or chemical interactions between the components of the wine. Sometimes both occur simultaneously.

Micro-organism haze or deposit
The easiest way of telling if a haze or deposit is due to the activity of yeasts or bacteria is to examine a drop of the wine or a little of the deposit under a microscope; for many people however, this will be impossible, and a different approach is therefore necessary.

(a) *Suspected yeast activity*
This can often be confirmed by taking a small amount of the hazy wine in a clean medicine bottle and adding a little sugar syrup, then after stoppering with a plug of cotton wool, putting the bottle in a warm place. If the next day the liquid is fermenting, almost certanly the haze in the main body of the wine is due to yeast activity. In addition to this, wines which have yeast growing in them usually have a characteristic aroma.

(b) *Suspected bacterial activity*
The aroma of the wine is nowhere near as indicative of

trouble as in the case of yeast, and a variation on the test described for yeast is necessary.

Two small glass bottles each of approximately 50 ml capacity must first be thoroughly cleaned and then sterilised by filling with water just off the boil. Sterilise the bottle tops by pouring some hot water into them. Leave to cool. Using a small filter funnel a filter paper is next folded, put into the funnel and this assembly is sterilised by running some nearly boiling water through it. Some of the wine is then filtered into each of the sterilised bottles and the tops are put on *loosely*. One of the bottles is then stood in nearly boiling water which is kept warm on the low heat of a cooker for 15–20 minutes. After allowing both bottles to cool to the same temperature, the tops are tightened down and then both are placed in a warm airing cupboard, after which they require examining at 3, 5 and 8 day intervals. If the unheated bottle shows a turbidity but the heated bottle remains clear. it indicates a bacterial infection to be the cause of the haze.

Both yeast and bacteria can be removed by filtration, but in either case a dose of 100 ppm of sulphur dioxide should be added to the *filtered* wine to retard any further micro-organism growth.

In the event of the haze not being due to either bacteria or yeast, a chemical explanation has to be sought.

Hazes and deposits of chemical origin

The most likely causes are as follows:

1. *Pectin.* This large molecule carbohydrate owes its origin to the fruit. It is best to ensure it does not present a problem by adding pectinase enzyme to the juice prior to fermentation; however the same tactic can be employed for finished wines. Many pectinase preparations are available and all that is necessary is to follow the directions given with the product chosen.

Before adding pectinase to a wine, make sure that the problem is due to pectin by taking a test tube and adding to it about 1 cm depth of the wine to be tested. To this add approximately 3 cm of methylated spirit and shake the tube, closing it with a finger. Put the tube to one side and examine it after about 15 minutes. If a white desposit or haze is present, pectin is the cause of the problem and pectinase enzyme treatment can go ahead.

2. *Starch.* Wines made from root vegetables are the most prone to this form of haze, although it is possible to experience it with wines made from dessert apples or pears. To check if this is the cause of a haze, simply take a little of the wine in a test tube and add a drop of iodine solution. If a blue colour develops, starch is the problem.

Removal of a starch haze can be easily accomplished by adding Amylase enzyme. Again, many preparations are on the market and it is only necessary to follow the directions on the enzyme bottle.

3. *Protein.* Young wines or those which have not fully matured sometimes throw a protein haze or desposit. In the case of a deposit, careful racking of the wine from the deposit into a clean vessel is the answer, but in the case of a haze, it is first necessary to carry out a test to confirm that protein is the most likely cause. This is done by using a large test tube or a small clear glass bottle and adding to it about 25 mls of the wine. To this is added 1.5 mls of 5% tannic acid solution (5 gms of tannic acid dissolved in 100 mls of water). A graduated pipette is useful for the tannic acid addition. If a cloudy or flocculent deposit is formed, it is likely that the cause of the haze is protein instability. A confirmatory test is then necessary.

Confirmatory test—to a 100 ml sample of the wine add 2 drops of 10% sodium metabisulphite solution (10 gms of sodium metabisulphite dissolved in 100 mls of water) followed by 1 ml of 5% bentonite solution. Mix well, seal the bottle or tube and stand for 24 hours or until settlement has taken place, then carefully decant a clear sample into a test tube and test with 5% tannic acid as described above. If no cloud or deposit is now formed the wine did have protein instability.

To treat protein instability, add to each 4.5 litres (1 gallon) of wine 45 mls of a 5% suspension of bentonite in the wine and mix thoroughly. Allow sufficient time to properly settle and then rack off into a clean vessel.

4. *Colour instability.* Young red wines often contain colouring matter which because of contact with air during the bottling operation, comes out of solution and forms a haze or

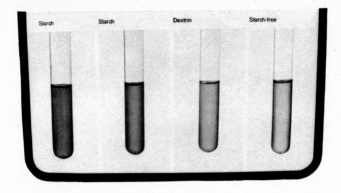

STARCH TEST

The tube on the far left shows the deep blue produced by high starch content in a wine, whereas the second tube shows a lesser quantity of starch. The pink/brown colour of the third tube shows the presence of partially degraded starch (dextrin); the tube on the far right, absence of starch.

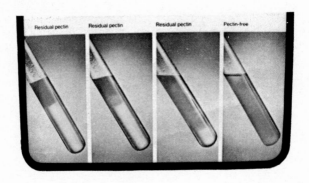

PECTIN TEST

The tube on the right shows a sample tested for pectin with methylated spirit and found to be pectin free. The other three tubes show varying amounts of pectin.

deposit. If a sample of the wine with such a haze or deposit is run through a filter paper the pigment is often easily seen when all the wine has run through. Such a wine can be stabilised by putting suitable size bottles containing the wine into a domestic refrigerator and leaving them there for three days and then carefully racking the wine, preferably with filtration, into clean bottles, adding about as much sodium metabisulphite as will cover the tip of a penknife—as shown in Fig. 3—to each bottle and then securely corking or capping as the case might be.

FIG. 3.

5. *Metal contamination.* If the wine has been allowed to come into contact with either iron, copper or zinc surfaces, a haze or deposit may be formed. Usually the taste and often the colour of the wine is also affected. It is beyond the means of the home winemaker to do anything about this, and regrettably such wine is usually best thrown away. It cannot be too strongly emphasised that wines should not be allowed to come into contact with *any* metal other than stainless steel, and that pewter drinking vessels must not be used because of the risk of lead extraction. This also applies to pottery not specifically sold as suitable for wine, as it can also have heavy metals in the glaze.

FILTRATION

Earlier in this chapter mention was made of filtration for the removal of micro-organisms, this involves the use of specially manufactured filter media which not very long ago was outside the scope of most home winemakers. Today, it is possible to remove, in the home, yeast and many of the bacteria which cause wine spoilage by filtration of an infected wine. Not all wines which have a haze or deposit require such fine filtration as that for micro-organism removal, and in many cases filtration is employed as part of the racking

27

operation to prevent any settled deposit or finings passing into the vessel receiving the bright wine. The following methods can all be used by the home winemaker, although as will be seen, there are special considerations associated with the different methods which cannot be neglected if good results are to be obtained.

Simple open funnel filtration

This, as its name implies, uses an open funnel made of either glass, plastic or stainless steel, into which has been placed a folded or fluted filter paper of appropriate size. A fluted paper gives a quicker throughput of wine, yet the same retention as folding a paper. Folding a paper is easy but fluting requires a little more practice.

To flute a paper circle, first make four folds so that the paper is divided into eight equal sectors (1), the two halves of the paper on each occasion being folded forwards, so that all

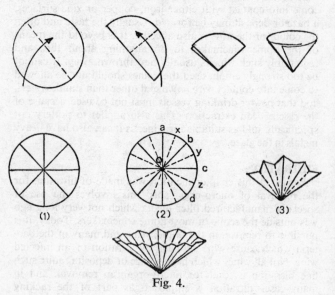

Fig. 4.

28

the folds tend to be concave. Now take each segment in turn (e.g. *aob*, (2)), and fold the points *ab* backwards until they meet, so that the *a* new convex fold *ox* is made between them: continue in this way, making new folds *oy*, *oz*, etc., around the paper. Ready to use fluted filter papers to fit funnels with a diameter of 12.5-50 cms are now available from laboratory suppliers.

Unless the funnel is extended the wine would cascade through the air in the jar, dissolving oxygen until a level is reached to submerge the outlet. This would result in premature browning of the wine and thus create a new problem. A simple solution is to fit to the outlet of the funnel a piece of suitable size tubing to take the filtered wine right to the bottom of the receiving vessel.

An alternative to using the conventional funnel with filter paper as just described, is to use an open top funnel provided with a support plate which is perforated with holes. On the support plate can be placed either a filter pad or a pulp made from torn up filter paper through which the cloudy wine can be filtered. Because of the support plate this type of funnel—which is more correctly termed a Buchner funnel—can be used with a suction pump to pull the wine through the filter. Both conventional funnel and Buchner funnel filtering arrangements are shown in the photograph facing page 29.

The suction type of filtration possible with the Buchner funnel requires other special equipment to make the operation safe and unlikely to implode due to working at less than atmospheric pressure. As will be seen from the photograph, a special receiving flask with a side arm and a trap in the tube, which is of heavy walled construction, along with a simple filter pump connected to a water tap comprises the assembly.

The filter media of either circular discs correctly sized to fit the funnel or torn up filter paper mixed with water to make a pulp is first put into the funnel on the support plate. If circular discs are used they must first be moistened with water. In either case, the funnel is then filled with water which has been boiled and then allowed to cool slightly, this is then pulled through the filter by slowly turning on the water tap to which the filter pump is fitted. The process is repeated several times to completely wash from the media any taint which might have been associated with the paper. The receiving flask can be emptied by turning off the water and removing the funnel. The hissing noise which will be heard is air entering the system' If a trap is not put in the tubing from the pump to the receiver every time the water is turned off, some water will be drawn back into the flask therefore diluting the wine.

Any open top filter funnel needs constant attention to top up as necessary and in addition to this, the vacuum system draws off from the wine being filtered some of its bouquet; a sealed type of filter is therefore more desirable than the open type and suction filtration avoided if possible.

Closed system filtration

There are now on the market many types of filter which can justifiably claim to operate on the closed system principle, some of them are very expensive, whilst others are relatively cheap. The following will provide a guide to the types available and their relative merits, so that the individual winemaker can make his or her own decision on which to purchase.

1. *Tube type filters.* The simplest form of this type of filter consists of a hollow cylinder of filter media 5.75 cm in length and 1.5 cm in diameter. Into one end is inserted a blank end stop of polypropylene and into the other end a connecting piece made of the same material. Because of its small diameter this type of filter will pass through the neck of most jars and bottles, and this makes it particularly useful when racking a wine which has a depsoit. Unfortunately, because of the small size, if the deposit is disturbed, or a heavy haze exists, the filter tubes are easily blocked. The arrangement for using one of these filters is shown in Fig. 5 and the media, which is made by Whatman, can be obtained from laboratory suppliers and home winemaking stockists.

A larger version of the simple tube filter described above is the Gamma 12, also made by Whatman. This uses cylinders 15.75 cm in length and 3.1 cm in diameter. The filter's capacity is therefore greater. It does not, however, have the ability to be inserted into the vessel from which filtration is taking place, and it requires a special plastic housing. Its advantages are that it is very compact, the housing is transparent and you

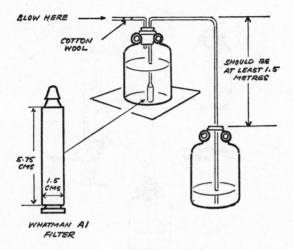

BLOW HERE

COTTON
WOOL

SHOULD BE
AT LEAST 1.5
METRES

5.75
CMS

1.5
CMS

WHATMAN A1
FILTER

FIG. 5.

can see if anything untoward happens. It is also possible to obtain media for this type of filter which will remove most micro-organisms likely to be found in wine. This type of filter can be used as shown in Fig. 6 allowing the receiver bottle to act as support for the filter.

To operate these tube type filters with a syphonic system of the type illustrated, a minimum of about 1 metre of head should be allowed.

2. *Supported filter sheet filters.* The essential difference between these and the tube type filters described earlier is that the filter sheet disc rests on a support and more often than not has a back support as well. The value of this is in preventing the filter to sag at the middle and concentrate all of the filtering effect at that point, and to make sure that the disc is located correctly before filtration begins. The general way in which these filters are constructed is shown in Fig. 7. Many branded makes are available and the illustration is not intended to show any particular one.

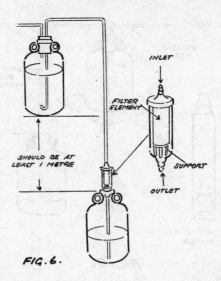

FIG. 6.

The filter disc is chosen to suit the purpose, viz., polishing, finings removal, or complete removal of yeast. Sheets for clarification are often numbered 1 to 10, the higher the number, the finer the degree of clarification. Yeast removing or so called sterilising sheets have a symbol S or some other designation. The correct grade must be chosen for the purpose intended or poor results will be achieved.

In setting up one of these filters the sequence of events is as follows:

1. Having chosen the grade of disc most suitable for the purpose intended, mount the disc on to the filter support with the finest textured side downwards. The reason for this is the filter manufacturer usually applies a special binding finish to the outlet side of the discs to prevent fibres detaching and passing into the wine. Next position the back support, and if it has to be screwed in, make sure that the disc is not displaced in the process.

2. Using water at about 60°C (140°F) make a syphon as shown in Fig. 5 but raise the end up to just below the surface

32

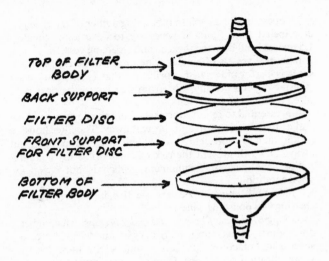

FIG. 7.

of the water and pinch it shut. Take the filter with the *exit* pointing upwards and connect the syphon tube to the inlet.

3. Slowly lower the whole filter assembly keeping the exit upwards until water flows out, then reverse the filter so that the exit points downwards into the receiver, and allow 4.5 litres (1 gallon) of warm water to pass through the filter and wash any taint out.

4. Some filters are fitted with an air vent, and in this case the filter can be joined straight away to the syphon tube, the air vent opened, the syphon made, as before, then when water starts to issue from the air vent it is shut and passage through the sheet commences.

5. When all the water has passed through the sheet, allow sufficient time for the syphon to drain completely, and then disconnect the filter and turn it upside down to drain out any water which may be left.

6. Transfer the syphon tube to the wine and repeat process for excluding air from the filter described in 2 and 3 or 4 above. The filter is then ready to operate with the wine.

To operate with a syphon tube using a filter of the type just described I have found it necessary to have approximately 1.5 metres head between the feed and receiving vessels.

If several vessels of similar wine are to be filtered and the sheet is performing satisfactorily, all that is necessary after transferring the racking tube from one jar to the next is to bleed the air from the system.

It is essential to remove the sheet from the apparatus at the end of the filtration run and throw it away. The filter housing should then be thoroughly washed and dried before being put away. This will prevent the risk of harbouring any contamination, and keep the equipment—which is not cheap—in good condition.

Filters of this type can be very effective, if properly used, for clearing and polishing wines.

3. *Supported sheet filters for use under pressure.* In commerce and industry, filters are usually operated under pressure, and several manufacturers produce a filter along these lines for small filtration operations. Care of course must be exercised using any apparatus under pressure, and the manufacturers' directions should be studied carefully and then followed.

Whilst it is difficult to force contamination through a filter operating with the syphonic system, using pressure this can occur more easily, particularly if the pressure is applied in bursts rather than as a consistent force.

This type of filter is good, but much more care is required in using it both in terms of operating and maintenance. They are also quite expensive. One such filter is shown in Fig. 8.

4. *Powder media filters.* This type of filter differs from the others which have been described, in that the filtration is achieved by making a slurry of a suitable powder and then depositing this on to a porous support. As the filter run progresses additional filter area is created by incorporating a proportion of the filter aid powder in the wine being fed to the filter. The initial coating of powder is called the Precoat, and the powder applied in the wine the Bodycoat.

Filters of this kind are used widely in industry but they require considerable skill if good results are to be obtained. The choice of powders, the operating conditions and the nature of the wine being filtered are all important. Failure to

34

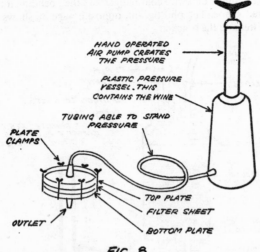

HAND OPERATED
AIR PUMP CREATES
THE PRESSURE

PLASTIC PRESSURE
VESSEL. THIS
CONTAINS THE WINE

TUBING ABLE TO STAND
PRESSURE

PLATE
CLAMPS

TOP PLATE

FILTER SHEET

OUTLET

BOTTOM PLATE

FIG. 8.

get the conditions right results in filter aid passing into the receiving vessel, and this of course, means the wine comes out of the filter with a haze.

Several small scale powder media filters are on sale at varying prices, and the results I have seen from them have not been encouraging.

5. *A home-made filter*. I wanted a filter which I could use with either a cellulose filter media or Kieselguhr, and which would operate on a continuous principle. My criteria was also that the construction should be easy and require only simple tools, and that the finished object would be robust and compact when stored.

With this in mind I decided to use a screw-top high density polythene jar for the body of the filter, as this could be easily drilled and dismantled. For the pipe connections I selected GKN Plasticon connectors with 6 mm (3/16") outside diameter tubing for the reason that they could be easily obtained from any large hardware supplier.

The filter was assembled as shown in Fig. 9, and a mounting bracket which could be hung on the wall, fashioned by

35

straightening out a wire coat hanger and then bending it to the desired shape. The photograph opposite page 36 shows both the filter and the bracket.

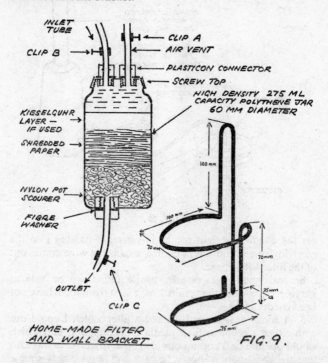

INLET TUBE

CLIP A

CLIP B

AIR VENT

PLASTICON CONNECTOR

SCREW TOP

HIGH DENSITY 275 ML CAPACITY POLYTHENE JAR 60 MM DIAMETER

KIESELGUHR LAYER — IF USED

SHREDDED PAPER

NYLON POT SCOURER

FIBRE WASHER

OUTLET

CLIP C

100 mm

100 mm

70 mm

70mm

35mm

75 mm

HOME-MADE FILTER AND WALL BRACKET

FIG. 9.

Filter media can be costly and after considerable experimentation I have found that if 3 sheets of uncoloured kitchen or Kleenex tissue is first torn into approximately 50 mm × 50 mm (2″ × 2″) squares and then shredded in a liquidiser such as a Braun, Kenwood or Krupp kitchen machine, a loose textured material is produced which is excellent for general filtration. If the user wishes to use Kieselguhr or another filter aid, then, after the initial runnings which need to be returned to the vessel feeding the filter, the filter aid will be retained on the surface of the paper pad, and assist in clearing the wine.

36

LIQUIDISER
A liquidiser which can be used for shredding paper for use as
a filter media.

Preparing the filter

After positioning a neutral coloured nylon pot scourer over the outlet of the filter to prevent the media blocking the outlet, the shredded paper is put into the pot and the top screwed on.

A small funnel is connected to the inlet tube and clips A and B are opened and clip C screwed shut.

Water at approximately 80°C is poured into the funnel until it just issues from the tube on which clip A is fixed. Clip A is then closed and clip C opened. About 500 mls of hot water is then flowed through the filter to wash and sterilise the assembly and media. After this volume has been passed the filter is allowed to drain through the outlet.

Filtering wine

A similar procedure is followed as for washing the filter except that the inlet tube is first connected to the racking or syphon tube which is dipping into the wine which is to be filtered, and the outlet is connected to the collecting vessel (see Fig. 10).

The air vent is opened by unscrewing clip A and a syphon made from the jar containing the wine to the filter, by blowing into the vent tube of the jar containing the wine with a small plug of cotton wool to act as an air filter. When wine just emerges from the air vent of the filter, clip A is closed and clip C half opened. Clip C is further adjusted to obtain a flow rate of about 500 mls/5 minutes. Filtration is then allowed to proceed until all the wine has been filtered.

When filtration is complete, close clip C, disconnect from the syphon tube and throw away the paper pulp and debris from the filter and wash it out.

Choice of filter media

For a long time a mixture of specially prepared cellulose and asbestos fibres has been used as a filter media. Filter sheets made of the same materials, fabricated using techniques employed in the paper industry are widely available and used in many industries.

The main reason for using asbestos is the high surface attraction properties which gives a filter sheet or coating an ability to retain particles and organisms which would not be

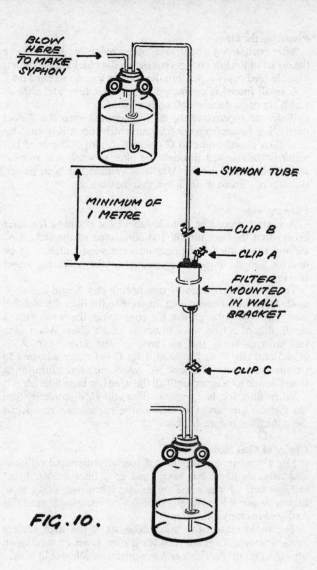

FIG. 10.

removed by the sieving effect of the filter. Over the years new materials have come on to the market, but asbestos is still important.

There is no doubt that inhalation of asbestos fibres can damage health, and there have been doubts expressed about the possible effects of asbestos fibres in liquids on health. It is for these reasons that I recommend the use of asbestos free filter sheets and powders for home winemaking purposes. Even then, care should be taken not to inhale any dust when using powders, to avoid any respiratory irritation.

FINING

This process, unlike filtration can be clarifying and/or purifying, and advantage can be taken from the purifying ability to remove colour as will be described later whilst the clarifying aspect can be used to either supplement or completely replace filtration.

Clarification

The choice of fining agent depends on what is causing the haze, or to be more exact, what electrical charge is on the particles of the haze.

To reduce the matter to simple proportions, only two fining agents will be considered:

1. *Bentonite*. This is a negatively charged fining which removes positively charged particles such as proteins. It is an excellent fining when properly used.

2. *Isinglass*. This is a positively charged fining and therefore used to remove negatively charged hazes. Other positively charged finings exist, but isinglass is perhaps the easiest for the home winemaker to use.

The problem is deciding if the haze in a wine is positively or negatively charged. Proteins whilst themselves positively charged, when they are linked to tannins (polyphenols) change the charge to negative. A practical solution is to apply a simple fining trial and from the result decide which fining will be best.

A simple fining trial

Prepare a 1 % solution of bentonite by taking 1 gm of

39

bentonite powder and sprinkling it into 100 mls of warm—not boiling—water. The bentonite will not dissolve, but if it is shaken regularly over the period of a day and immediately before it is used, a good suspension will be obtained.

A 1% solution of isinglass will also be required. To do this, soak 1 gm of isinglass in 25 mls of water overnight. Next day add water to bring the volume up to 100 mls, and stir well.

The only other solution required is 1% tannic acid. Pharmaceutical grade should be purchased; simply dissolve 1 gm of the tannic acid in 100 mls of water.

The procedure is then as follows: Take 6 jars or glasses of approximately the same size made of clear glass, and measure into each 100 mls of the wine. Using a 5 ml graduated pipette, add 0.5, 1.0, 1.5, 2.0, 2.5 and 3.0 mls of the 1% bentonite suspensions to the jars or glasses respectively. Immediately after the addition of the fining to a jar or glass, shake the vessel and label it so that next day it is clear which concentration of fining has been used. On the following day examine the vessels carefully without disturbing them, and look for the one giving a clear bright wine for the smallest addition of bentonite. In this way overfining will be avoided.

The trial results are easily converted so that an addition can be made to the bulk of the wine. Simply measure the volume of wine to be fined in mls and divide by 100 then multiply by the number of mls of bentonite which gave the best result from the fining trial. For example:

If the fining trial had shown 1.5 mls to give the best result and 4250 mls of wine is to be fined, the quantity of 1% bentonite to add would be $\dfrac{4250}{100} \times 1.5 = 63.75$ mls. The amount of bentonite contained in this volume of 1% suspension is easily calculated by dividing the number of mls by 100,

i.e. $\dfrac{63\cdot75}{100} = 0.6375$ gms, to 2 decimal places, 0.64 gms. This quantity of bentonite has then to be weighed out and shaken up in some of the *wine* and this then added to the bulk of the wine and well mixed in.

In simple terms: Number of gms. of fining required for each

litre of wine=the number of mls. of 1 % fining most satisfactory in the 100 ml. fining trial divided by 10.

If bentonite is unsuccessful in clarifying the wine, the chances are isinglass will clarify it, and to ascertain the quantity required a fining trial will need to be carried out in exactly the same way as that described for bentonite, but using 1 % isinglass. There is a complication, isinglass removes tannin and because of this it is necessary to add the same amount of 1 % tannic acid to the 100 ml volumes of the wine as isinglass, viz, 1 ml of isinglass then 1 ml of 1 % of tannic acid as well. Establish which addition, e.g., 0.5, 0.1, 1.5, etc., mls gives the best clarity and calculate the addition of fining per litre of wine in the same way as for bentonite, (i.e. number of mls of 1 % fining most satisfactory in the 100 ml fining trial, divided by 10=gms of fining/litre).

COLOUR ADJUSTMENT

There will inevitably arise occasions when the wine colour does not match up to expectation. Many people have come to regard this as something of a disaster, but this need not be the case. It is a relatively simple matter to reduce the colour of a white or red wine, or if necessary increase the density of the colour tint for red or white wines by the use of food grade approved colouring materials or deeply coloured wines specially prepared for the purpose.

Colour removal

Both activated carbon and casein have strong colour removing properties. Unfortunately both have problems associated with their use. Carbon has such high activity that the quantity necessary to treat 4.5 litres (1 gallon) of wine is usually so small that an accurate balance is called for. Casein on the other hand is a difficult material to dissolve. Fortunately there is an easy answer. Milk contains casein and can therefore be used for colour removal. The technique is to use only skimmed milk, or milk from which the cream has been carefully removed. A fining trial is set up in the same way as that described for bentonite on page 40 using 0.5, 1.0, 1.5 and 2.0 mls of milk. The glasses are left overnight and the glass containing the wine with the colour nearest to that intended, indicates the amount of milk as a percentage for the whole volume. Thus, if the 1.5 ml glass gave the best result, 15 mls of milk would be required to treat a litre of the wine, and multiples of this can be taken for any other quanity of wine involved, viz. 4.5 litres requires $15 \times 4.5 = 67.5$ mls.

Having decided how much milk is required to remove the colour to the desired level in a known quantity of wine, it is necessary first to measure out the quantity of milk to be mixed into the bulk of the wine, and then well agitate the wine whilst adding the milk to it. This avoids what is known as localised fining, and ensures that the colour removal effect is spread throughout the volume of the wine being treated. After the addition of the fining it is important to make sure that a headspace does not exist above the wine, or excessive contact with air may occur. The vessel should be topped up with either a little wine of a similar style and character to that which is being treated, or if no wine is available, a little boiled and cooled water which will then need to be mixed into the bulk. A slight dilution will occur if the water technique is employed, but this is preferable to allowing contact with air and possible development of surface growing micro-organisms which would lead to product spoilage. After topping up, the wine should be well stoppered and set aside for the fining to settle. When the fining has settled on the bottom of the vessel, rack the clear supernatant wine into a clean sterilised vessel. The Fig. 11 shows how a syphon can be made by blowing through a tube containing a small plug of cotton wool, passing through the bung alongside the racking tube. This technique applies a downward pressure on the surface of the wine and pushes it through the racking tube to make a syphon. By this method no part of the tubing through which wine will flow comes in contact with the mouth. It also allows the racking tube to start the transfer of wine at the bottom of the fresh vessel; at no time is wine, therefore, allowed to cascade through the air. Instead entry of the wine into the second vessel displaces air from it progressively as the transfer takes place: excessive contact with air is thus avoided.

Dried milk

There is now available on the market a powdered skimmed

42

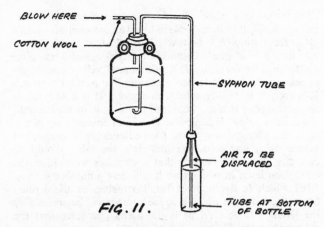

FIG. 11.

milk of high quality which, when reconstituted with water makes an excellent milk fining agent. A trial can be performed in exactly the same way as that described for fresh milk and the dried product has the advantage of having a much longer life than fresh milk—a useful consideration for the winemaker who might want skimmed milk at short notice.

MAKING GOOD COLOUR DEFICIENCIES

Sometimes wines turn out paler than intended or desired. In the case or red wines, although the colour tone might be correct, the depth may not be. In cases such as these it is possible to blend the pale wine with a little wine of a deeper colour to improve the appearance. Whilst this sounds a simple enough procedure, there are complications. Often a wine of greater colour depth is not available, or alternatively the wine available is of a completely different character to the wine which needs to be corrected. Another problem is that when two wines are blended together chemical reactions sometimes take place between the colouring, protein, tannin and other complex substances present to produce a haze or deposit a short time after the mixing operation.

White wines

It is difficult to correct a pale white wine by blending in another wine of greater colour density because frequently a deep colour in a white wine is synonymous with oxidation, and obviously it is undesirable to blend an oxidised wine into a clean fresh wine. All, however, is not lost. It is possible to purchase a food grade colouring material called Tartrazine. In the powder form this is a pronounced yellow and might appear to the inexperienced eye more like a paint pigment. However, it is readily soluble in water and if a solution is made, drops of this can be added to the bulk of a wine until the desired colour is achieved. This is, of course, only of use for white wines. Other yellow food colours are available, but before using any colouring materials, the label should be carefully checked to ensure that it complies with either the EEC food laws, in which case it will bear a number such as E102 which is the number for Tartrazine, or the United States food laws, in which case the number will be prefixed by the letters FD & C. This is the user's guarantee that the colouring material is suitable for food or beverage use.

Ready made solutions of some food grade colours are available, and in such cases it is likely that the solution will contain glycerine (or glycerol), propylene glycol, propyl alcohol or ethyl alcohol. These substances all act as preservatives and prevent deterioration of the colouring solution.

Red wines

With red wines greater scope exists for colour adjustments. Frequently another darker wine can be added to a colour deficient wine, not only improving the colour, but often the flavour as well.

Elderberry wine provides the ideal deep coloured wine with which to make colour adjustments, and all wine makers should prepare some of this wine for this purpose, if for no o her reason. The secret is to keep the quantity of water used down to a minimum so that the resultant wine is very rich in colour. A good recipe is as follows:

ELDERBERRY WINE

Elderberries	3 kilos
Sugar	1.5 kilos
Ammonium sulphate	3 grammes
Sodium metabisulphite	1.5 grammes
Citric acid	15 grammes
Pectic enzyme	According to manufacturer's directions
Water	4.5 litres
Active yeast culture	

44

The berries should be stripped from the stalks using a fork, and then crushed in a bowl. On to this is poured boiling water; the volume of water boiled needs to be measured to ensure that the overall recipe is kept at 4.5 litres of added water. The berries and the hot water are thoroughly mixed together, and to this is added the sugar followed by more mixing to ensure that the sugar is completely dissolved. The mixture is allowed to cool till the bowl can be comfortably held in the hands, and at this point the rest of the ingredients, with the exception of the yeast, is added, and yet another mixing carried out. The yeast is then added, the mixture stirred, and divided between two jars, each of 4.5 litres capacity. Each jar is loosely stoppered with cotton wool moistened with sodium metabisulphate solution and set aside for fermentation to commence. For the next three days the jars need to be stirred each day, and then on the third day of fermentation the contents of both jars transferred to a third jar via a funnel containing a muslin pulp filter. The third jar should be filled to the base of the neck and a fermentation lock inserted to keep the fermenting wine out of contact with the air. The fermentation is then allowed to complete in a warm place away from direct sunlight. When fermentation has ceased, the wine is racked into bottles, tightly corked and set aside in the *dark* for use as colour blending wine.

Elderberry wine develops with time, both in flavour and colour, the latter becoming a deep mahogany shade. When the wine has reached this state of maturity it is usually so good that winemakers are reluctant to use it as colour blending wine and prefer to retain it for drinking on a special occasion. This great temptation must be overcome by the winemaker who wishes to use a wine specially prepared for colour adjustment purposes.

Beetroot wine is another good source of colour, but the wine itself is more coarse and does not contribute much by way of bouquet or flavour when added to another wine. In colour terms it is more blue-red than Elderberry which has matured for approximately the same period of time. Unless Beetroot wine is kept away from contact with the light, it tends to darken and become brown in colour and storage of Beetroot wine must therefore be done either in complete darkness or in jars which are brown in colour, and stored away from the light. For those who wish to make Beetroot wine the following recipe might be of interest:

BEETROOT WINE

Beetroot	1.5 kilos
Sugar	1.5 kilos
Citric acid	15 grammes
Water	4.5 litres
Ammonium phosphate	3 grammes
Amylase enzyme	As directed on the preparation used
Active yeast culture	

The beetroots need to be washed well to remove any earth but should not be peeled. Dicing is the best way to prepare them followed by boiling in the water until tender, but not reduced to a mash. At this stage the sugar, acid, ammonium phosphate and any remaining water is added, and the mixture stirred until the sugar has been dissolved. The liquid is then allowed to cool. At this point the amylase enzyme added, and the mixture left for a further one hour. After this period, the yeast culture is added, the mixture stirred and the vessel covered with a muslin cloth which has been wrung out in 1% sodium metabisulphite solution to keep it free from any bacteria or yeast. The fermentation is allowed to proceed in this way for three days and then the liquid is strained from the pulp using a muslin pulp filter contained in a funnel and the fermentation completed in a 4.5 litre glass jar closed with a fermentation lock in the usual manner. As mentioned previously, it is important that this glass jar should be protected from light or the colour of the wine will be lost. When the fermentation has ceased, 1.5 gms of metabisulphite is added to the wine, and after leaving for 24 hours for resettlement of the lees, the clear wine is bottled and tightly corked for future use as colour blend stock.

Where no blending wine exists the only alternative is to resort to food grade colouring materials, and in the case of red wines choice can hardly be said to be very great, the choices being Cochineal (E120), Amaranth (E123), Beetroot red (E162) and Enocyanin (E163).

Cochineal, once found in many kitchens will impart a

delicate light cherry red colour to a wine, whilst Amaranth will contribute a deeper red/blue tinge.

Cochineal (E120) is still available as a ready prepared solution and can be purchased at pharmacies, grocers, or herbalists. Amaranth (E123) is a highly concentrated food grade colour in powder form which needs to be made into a solution by mixing a small quantity with water. Such a solution can then be used a drop at a time to bring up the colour of a wine which is not as full as expected or desired.

Beetroot Red (E162), an aqueous extract from Beetroot can be used in the same way as Amaranth solution, and is supplied ready to use in liquid form. A little more difficulty may be found in obtaining this colouring material than for the other two mentioned above.

Enocyanin (E163) is the natural colour extracted from red grape skins and can be added as a powder or dissolved in water and added dropwise as described for Amaranth.

Light fastness

All colours suffer to a lesser or greater extent from exposure to ultra violet light. The greatest natural source of such light is the sun, and therefore wines should be kept out of the direct path of sunlight if their colour is to be preserved. This is very important and often overlooked by home winemakers, with the result, that when they come to take out a wine which at the last inspection was a very good colour, they find deterioration has taken place, and what was a deep red is now rather a dull brown, or what was a delicate pale straw is now almost water white. This point cannot be too strongly emphasised.

CHAPTER 3

IMPROVING THE BOUQUET

SINCE aroma is normally perceived shortly after appraisal of a wine's clarity and colour, obviously it is important to give the wine as good a bouquet as possible.

Despite a lot of effort put into balancing the raw materials for fermentation, careful conduct of the fermentation and speed of racking from the lees, a wine can still turn out rather lacking in aroma.

On the other hand, sometimes a fermentation does not give the clean finish hoped for, and an off aroma develops. This chapter describes how some of these problems can be overcome.

Removing off aroma

Quite often if an off aroma is present it is due to nothing more than dissolved gases, the by-products of fermentation. If therefore, the unpleasant smelling gas can be removed, the problem disappears and the wine aroma is cleansed.

Generally speaking, wines suitable for treatment by sparging have a smell either of sulphur or rotten eggs (hydrogen sulphide). Chemicals called Mercaptans are frequently involved and the origin of the aroma due to wine in contact with metals or fermentation defects.

(a) *Gas sparging*

Sparging consists simply of cascading the wine through air or bubbling a gas—usually carbon dioxide or nitrogen— through the wine.

(i) CASCADING THROUGH AIR

This can be simply done by decanting the wine from one vessel to another. Fig. 12 shows such a simple sparging.

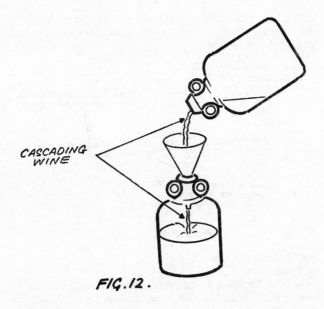

CASCADING WINE

FIG. 12.

(ii) BUBBLING

The home winemaker has at his or her disposal carbon dioxide from fermentation, this can be used to sparge a wine with off aroma. A set up for doing this is shown in Fig. 13.

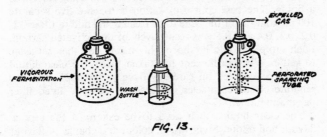

VIGOROUS FERMENTATION

WASH BOTTLE

EXPELLED GAS

PERFORATED SPARGING TUBE

FIG. 13.

The wash bottle between the fermentation vessel and the wine to be sparged gives the carbon dioxide gas a wash

49

before it is used for sparging through a plastic syphon tube drilled with numerous small holes. Fig. 14 shows how such a tube can be easily made.

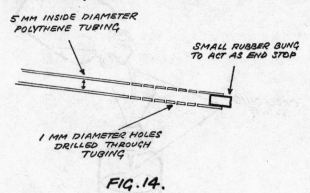

5 MM INSIDE DIAMETER POLYTHENE TUBING

SMALL RUBBER BUNG TO ACT AS END STOP

1 MM DIAMETER HOLES DRILLED THROUGH TUBING

FIG. 14.

(b) *Chemical treatment*
(i) CARBON

Activated carbon of the highest purity should be used to ensure that no undesirable impurities exist which could be extracted by the wine to which it is subsequently added.

Off aroma and off flavour characteristics are adsorbed on to the surface of the carbon particles which are in an activated state due to heat treatment. Because of the high state of activation, great care must be exercised when using carbon as a fining. The best course of action is to take five separate 100 ml volumes of the wine to be treated and add to these 0.1, 0.2, 0.3, 0.4 and 0.5 gms respectively of the activated carbon. Each sample should be thoroughly mixed and then set aside to settle. When settlement has taken place, the clear liquid should be decanted off carefully from each sample into five separate clean receptacles, if necessary using a fluted filter paper and funnel.

The clear liquids then need to be examined for aroma, flavour and odour. Some loss of colour and change of flavour as well as clean up of aroma is inevitable. Whilst the flavour might vary from being more clean to losing some of its high-lights, the colour intensity will be reduced. Obviously no more carbon than is absolutely necessary should be used, and the sample showing the best result for the lowest weight of carbon added is the treatment selected for the bulk of the wine.

Never add activated carbon to a wine without carrying out a trial, or the resultant wine may turn out lacking in flavour and aroma and water white in colour.

(ii) SULFIDEX (SULFEX)

This proprietary product is of West German origin, and consists of colloidal silver chloride mixed with Kieselguhr. It is expensive but very effective in removing the aroma of hydrogen sulphide or mercaptans from wine. As a generality, 0.5–1.0 gms/litre of wine is usually sufficient, but it is possible that a really bad off odour will require more.

After using Sulfidex, the wine must be set aside to settle, then racked, leaving the deposit behind. The resultant wine then needs to be bentonite fined to remove any residual silver salt, followed by settlement, and racking.

(iii) POLYVINYLPOLYPYRROLIDONE (PVPP)

This chemical is sold under the proprietary name Polyclar A.T. Where browning exists in a white wine, there is always a possibility of an aroma defect developing fairly soon. PVPP removes polyphenols and tannins which brown in the presence of air, and at the same time produce changes in aroma and flavour. A dose of 0.3–0.5 gms of PVPP per litre of wine is usually sufficient to remove this risk. It should be left in contact with the wine for a minimum time of 30 minutes and then filtered off. No problems will arise if the contact time is extended for longer than 30 minutes.

(c) *Yeast fining*

This is a procedure which is not very well covered in the many books published on the subject of wine, probably because of the relatively long time necessary for it to be effective.

The procedure is to prepare a vigorous culture of yeast in a juice of similar origin to that from which the wine exhibiting off aroma was fermented. An addition of the yeast culture of approximately 10% of the wine volume to be treated is added and well mixed in. The yeast must be left in contact with the wine for one to two weeks after which time the wine is racked and filtered if necessary, followed by bentonite fining, as has been previously described.

The action of this type of fining is largely that of adsorption on the surface of the yeast cells which are then deposited along with the agents causing off flavour and aroma. It has been suggested that certain amino acids added to a wine reduce any off odours or flavours present, and since yeasts contribute some of these substances this may be a secondary action.

Aroma addition

The first sections of this chapter have described how the aroma, or bouquet of a wine can be improved by the removal of unpleasant features. Sometimes, after such treatment the whole bouquet has been flattened, and it is desirable to put back some of the aroma character to make the wine balanced and attractive in terms of the three senses of sight, smell and taste.

Wines made from ingredients low in aroma can also lack bouquet.

Ideally a blend of a low aroma wine with a wine of similar character but good aroma, is the best way of correcting an aroma deficiency and this, in fact, is the standard practice of commercial winemakers who are handling wines all made from grapes. It is much more unlikely for a home winemaker to have at his or her disposal, wine of the correct colour, style, and character for such a blending at any particular moment in time. A good plan for any winemaker is therefore to prepare a few wines for the express purpose of blending to improve the aroma of other wines which may be lacking in this respect. Raspberry, Elderflower, and Rose Petal are three wines which are particularly useful in this context. The following recipes have been tried and found to give wines of particularly strong aroma and have proved useful for blending purposes.

RASPBERRY WINE

Raspberries (fresh)	4 kilos
Sugar	¾ kilo (750 grammes)
Sodium metabisulphite	1.5 grammes
Pectinase enzyme	As directed by the manufacturer
Water	to 4.5 litres
Active yeast culture	

First of all crush the raspberries, or better still, liquidise them in a high-speed liquidiser (see photograph facing page 37).

Transfer the crushed or liquidised fruit to a 4.5 litre glass fermentation jar using a funnel, and add the pectinase enzyme according to the particular manufacturer's directions on the product used. Add ½ litre of boiled and cooled water, and to the water add ½ gramme of sodium metabisulphite. Mix the contents of the jar thoroughly and add the yeast culture. Insert a fermentation lock in the neck of the jar and set it aside to ferment in a warm place, away from sunlight for three days. After this time, transfer the contents of the jar via a funnel and straining bag to a second clean and sterilised 4.5 litre fermentation vessel. This will remove most of the solids from the wine and the rest of the fermentation will therefore be conducted off of the pulp which has now been removed.

Dissolve ¾ kilo of sugar (sucrose) in ¾ litre of water by warming the water and adding the sugar until a clear syrup has been obtained. Allow the syrup to cool, and then add it to the fermenting juice. Finally top up the jar with boiled and cooled water and agitate the contents to mix well. Replace the fermentation lock in the neck of the jar and allow the fermentation to complete in a warm spot as before.

When the fermentation has completed, rack the wine into a clean and sterile jar and taste it to check the acidity is sufficiently high, if not, add some citric acid with mixing until the taste is sufficiently acid and then add 1 gramme of sodium metabisulphite. Top up the vessel with boiled and cooled water, mix and stopper. Set the wine aside to mature for six months, then bottle.

This wine is very full in aroma and flavour and can be blended with other more neutral wines to produce a wine of very acceptable character. Alternatively, a little of the raspberry wine can be added to a white wine to improve the bouquet and give a rosé style colour. For red wines, the aroma of the raspberry wine can prove very helpful in improving those which would otherwise be lacking in bouquet.

ELDERFLOWER WINE

Elderflowers (pressed down)	½ litre
Sugar	1.5 kilos
Sodium metabisulphite	1.5 grammes
Citric acid	25 grammes
Ammonium phosphate	2 grammes
Water	to 4.5 litres
Active yeast culture	

The flowers should be picked on a dry day and left in a container open to the air. Storage in a plastic bag can turn the promised delight of the flowers into disgust when the wine is made due to the development of a "catty" aroma. Similarly, the flowers should be smelt at the time of picking to be sure that no off aroma exists.

Trim the flowers from the stems with a pair of scissors until the right volume is achieved, remembering to pack down the flowers before measuring the volume. Transfer the flowers to a 4.5 litre fermentation jar.

Boil the water, allow it to cool slightly and then pour it over the flowers. Add to the water and the flowers, the sugar, followed by the citric acid and then ½ gramme of the sodium metabisulphite. Thoroughly mix the contents of the jar together, and allow them to cool to about 20°C (70°F), and then add the ammonium phosphate followed by the yeast. Insert a fermentation lock in the neck of the jar and allow fermentation to proceed in a warm place for five days. After this period, strain off the flowers by transferring the liquid through a funnel and strainer into a clean sterilised jar. Replace the fermentation lock, and allow the fermentation to complete,

When fermentation has ceased, rack the wine into a clean and sterile jar and add a further 1 gramme of sodium metabisulphite before re-stoppering the jar and allowing the wine to mature for three months, after which time, it may be bottled.

This wine is excellent for blending in small quantities into other aroma-deficient wines.

ROSE PETAL WINE

Rose petals (fresh, and of the strongest scent possible)	2 litres (packed down)
Sugar	1.25 kilos
Citric acid	25 grammes
Sodium metabisulphite	1.5 grammes
Ammonium phosphate	2 grammes
Water	to 4.5 litres

Active yeast culture

Proceed in the same way as that described for elderflower wine.

Again, this wine is excellent for blending to improve the aroma of other wines.

If no blending wine exists, it may be necessary to resort to the use of flavouring materials in concentrated form.

Use of added flavourings

There are now available on the market quite a large range of flavouring materials, some of which are intended to alter the character of a wine as well as change its aroma/flavour, so that a form of liqueur can be produced. Others are straight forward flavouring materials for addition to wine to improve the bouquet and/or flavour characteristics.

A word of caution must be added at this stage; many countries have labelling laws requiring flavouring compounds to have on their label a list of the ingredients in *descending* order in which they are present. Thus a liquid flavouring shown to have isopropyl alcohol and lemon oil extract in that order, would have a greater proportion of isopropyl alcohol than lemon oil extract. The reason for this is easily explained. Isopropyl alcohol is a solvent for many flavouring substaces, and it is necessary for it to be present in a relatively large amount. Some flavourings however, are shown on the label to contain fruit juice of one kind or another in addition to isopropyl alcohol and the chemical flavouring substances. This means sugar would be added to any wine to which such a flavouring was added and this will mean such a wine will be less stable and more susceptible to yeast growth. There is, therefore, a strong case for using flavourings whenever possible which do not contain fruit juices.

The aromas and flavours normally encountered in fermented beverages arise either from the starting materials, largely of botanical origin, or during the course of fermentation. Many flavouring substances suitable for addition to wine, are also therefore of botanical origin and are obtained by macerating the appropriate part of the plant in a solvent. However, this is not the only source of flavourings, as it is often possible to identify a chemical which will produce the bouquet or flavouring, and then use this instead of a botanical extract. A typical example of this kind of flavouring is Almond, which is easily produced by the use of benzaldehyde, thus making the use of costly almond extract unnecessary. When any flavouring is to be added to a wine, a check should first be made with a small sample to be sure that the flavouring mixes with the wine to form a homogeneous liquid and does not float on the surface. Flavourings containing essential oils are particularly prone to this kind of separation. Other flavourings can produce a slight haze in the wine to which they have been added, and this also should be avoided. There is no easy way of knowing if a wine will produce either of these phenomena because of the variation in chemical make-up between wines of different origins, and the chemical components of the flavouring additive. A simple trial is therefore essential.

A trace of a concentrated flavouring can impart an improvement to an aroma deficient wine whilst a higher dose will alter the flavour and aroma.

Experimentation is essential to get the best from added flavourings.

CHAPTER 4

GETTING THE TASTE BALANCE RIGHT

So far, ways of making wines more acceptable in terms of sight and smell have been dealt with; now comes the all important consideration of the taste.

Taste perception involves different areas of the tongue, mouth and throat, each receiving a particular stimuli the magnitude of each being combined by the brain to produce the overall taste response. Acidity, fruit flavour, sweetness, heat and weight in the mouth are important in the taste assessment process and in many ways can be controlled by the winemaker.

Each of the principle taste factors are dealt with in this chapter.

SWEETNESS

The first sip of a wine quickly tells the taster if it is sweet, dry or somewhere in between. What requires critical judgement is if that sweetness is properly balanced with the acidity and other taste charactersitics of the wine.

Sweet wines lacking in acidity are "flabby" whereas dry, very acid wines feel as if they are stripping the skin off the taster's mouth. Neither condition is uncommon and both can be corrected.

Another problem which can be experienced is that of an otherwise well balanced wine lacking a little body or weight in the mouth. Sugar addition in these circumstances, whilst giving body, would almost certainly upset the balance and an alternative is therefore required.

Last, but by no means least, there are wines which require sugar addition to provide the necessary balance and this can be added in a variety of ways, each giving a different flavour.

(a) Over-sweet wine

The most obvious way of dealing with this situation is to blend the over-sweet wine with another dryer wine which

57

would benefit from added sweetness. Alternatively, a vigorous starter yeast culture can be added and the fermentation re-started to reduce the sugar level.

If neither of the above alternatives is practical, more drastic action can be taken by simply diluting the wine with boiled and cooled water until a satisfactory level of sweetness is obtained and then the acidity re-adjusted to provide the correct balance.

(b) *More sweetness needed*

If straight sweetness combined with increased mouth weight is required, a syrup of cane sugar (sucrose) is the best material to use. Dissolving sugar crystals direct into a wine is a great temptation; it is not as practical, however, as making syrup by dissolving sugar in as little hot water as possible to obtain a concentrated solution which, when cooled, still flows easily and can be added, drop wise if necessary, to obtain the precise level of sweetness required.

Should sweetness with the minimum of added mouth weight be required, fructose—sometimes called fruit sugar—is the best choice. Weight for weight this sugar has 1.5 times the sweetening power of sucrose and can therefore produce the desired level of sweetness from a smaller sugar addition than would be required if cane sugar were used. Again the easiest way of controlling the sugar addition is to prepare a syrup. In cost terms, fructose is much more expensive than cane sugar, and its use, therefore, needs to be restricted to those occasions when its special properties are required.

(c) *Sweetness and flavour modification required*

When the sweetness needs to be increased along with the introduction of some flavour characteristics, the way is open for the use of honey and/or a concentrated fruit juice. The flavour of honey depends upon the source from which the bees have extracted the nectar and advantage can be taken of the many different types of honey available to introduce flavour along with sweetness when this is desired. The mixture of sugars present in honey contains glucose and fructose so once again the quantity necessary to produce quite a perceptive change in sweetness is rather less than would be expected if cane sugar were being used. Many delightful subtle flavours can be introduced, depending upon the choice of honey. For those who have not previously used honey, a relatively cheap way of gaining experience of the various flavours is to purchase a pack of miniature jars then if one of them is found to be just the right flavour, a large size jar of that one can be bought. Unfortunately honey can be rather expensive.

Another way of adding sweetness and flavour is to employ a concentrated fruit juice such as grape, blackcurrant, raspberry, apple or pear. Citrus fruit concentrates are lower in sugar content and not suitable for sweetening purposes. Grape juice concentrates can be obtained from many different types of grape, each with its own individual flavour characteristics and for this reason the choice must rest with the winemaker as no broad guidelines can be drawn to describe anything as elusive as the flavour differences likely to be encountered. However, there are some general principles:

(i) The highest concentration of juice available should be used for sweetening purposes. Usually this means eight or nine times the strength of the original juice, By insisting on this, small additions of concentrated juice can be made to the wine to produce increased sweetness.

(ii) Any concentrate which has a "cooked fruit" or cara-melised aroma should not be used for sweetening as the smell would affect the wine to which it is added.

(iii) Powerfully flavoured and coloured concentrates such as blackcurrant or raspberry (B.P.C. syrup of either is available at most chemists) can be used to provide not only sweetness and flavour but also colour addition. The amount of such a concentrate added, of course, needs to be carefully controlled so as not to upset the wine flavour and any remaining sweetness deficiency can then be made good by cane sugar addition.

(d) *Sweetness without sugar*

Glycerine (Glycerol) is a thick heavy liquid with a sweet taste and is naturally produced as one of the by-products of fermentation. It is, in fact, the substance largely responsible for the "tears" often seen on a glass containing dessert wine or liqueur. Addition of this material will improve the body of a wine at the same time increasing the sweetness to some degree but to nothing like the extent of that produced by sugar (either cane or fructose) addition.

Body (or mouth weight)

Under the heading of Sweetness, various ways of increasing the body or mouth weight of wine, whilst increasing the sweetness, have been given. There are, however, occasions when only the mouth weight or body needs to be increased without the addition of sweetness; for this purpose Dextrin syrup is the answer. Dextrin syrup resembles, in appearance, glycerine in that it is water white and very viscous. Chemically it is the half way stage between starch and sugar. Adding some of the syrup to a wine increases its body without altering the perceived sweetness and if small additions are made, accompanied by tasting, the body can be adjusted as desired.

All of the sugars in honey and fruit concentrates, together with cane sugar and fructose will, given time and the presence of yeast, ferment. It is therefore essential to protect the treated wine to prevent this occurring, and details of how to do this are given in Chapter 6.

ACIDITY

Poor acid balance is as obvious as lack of body or over-sweetness.

All wines must have some acidity regardless of the style— without it, sweet wines would be cloying and dry wines would lack the briskness and refreshing qualities which make them attractive. Apart from the taste aspects, acidity is important in giving a wine keeping properties. However, excessive acidity, whilst imparting greater resistance to the growth of yeast and bacteria, alters the taste characteristics so much as to make a wine virtually undrinkable. A balance of acidity is therefore essential, not enough to be objectionable, yet not so little that it fails to be perceived as one of the essential features of the flavour profile.

Lack of acidity

This is most often seen in wines of dessert style or those made from fruit or other raw materials low in acidity.

Correction is relatively easy after having first established the type of acid character necessary. The following provides a guide to what characteristics different acids can impart.

(a) *Lactic acid*

Found as the principal acid in sour milk, this has a smoother effect on the palate than other acids used for correction of wine. Normally it is sold as a 50% solution. Its keeping properties are not as good as those of the solid crystalline acids.

Red wines with a slight acid deficiency can be very effectively adjusted by the addition of lactic acid until the taste is considered correct.

(b) *Citric acid*

All citrus fruits contain citric acid, and compared to lactic acid the effect on the palate is more brisk and fresh. It is one of the most popular acids used by home winemakers, who in the main use crystals of citric acid monohydrate. White wines of medium to dry sweetness benefit by the use of citric acid to correct any lack of acidity as it gives them vitality and zest.

(c) *Tartaric acid*

The principal acid of the grape. Weight for weight it is about 1.6 times more acidic than citric acid, and somewhat tart or sharp in its effect on the palate. It is therefore excellent where such characteristics are required. Sparkling wines in particular benefit from their acidity being adjusted with tartaric acid.

Unfortunately there are problems in using tartaric acid which cannot be overlooked. When calcium or potassium is available for salt formation, tartaric acid combines to form either calcium tartrate, a salt of low solubility which therefore quickly crystalises from the wine, or potassium hydrogen tartrate, a half salt whose solubility is to a large extent dependent on temperature, as a result a wine which is clear and bright, can with a drop in temperature, suddenly throw a crystaline deposit of the salt. Not only is this unsightly but it also necessitates decanting the wine from the deposit accompanied by some loss of otherwise good wine.

(d) *Malic acid*

This is the acid responsible for the acidity present in apple

61

juice, it is also found in many other fruits but in smaller quantities. On a weight for weight basis it is approximately 1.25 times more acid on the palate than citric.

The taste effect is sour and tart. Under favourable circumstances bacterial degradation of malic acid can occur. During this process the acidity drops and carbon dioxide gas is given off, exactly the opposite of what is desired.

Apple wines benefit best by the addition of malic acid to improve their acidities.

(e) *Orthophosphoric acid*
Unlike the other acids which have been described, this is a mineral acid whereas they are organic. This means it does not have carbon in its basic structure; instead it has phosphorous. It has about 6 times greater acidity in comparison to citric acid, and therefore a small volume of the acid shifts the acidity of a wine to quite a marked degree and great care therefore needs to be exercised not to overdo the addition.

The chief virtue of this acid is that a few drops of it will adjust the pH of a wine with very little effect on the taste. This is dealt with again in Chapter 5.

Blending wines to increase acidity
Another way of dealing with a lack of acidity is to blend a low acidity wine with a similar wine of high acidity.

The high acidity wine should always be added to the one with low acid, and not vice versa so that the addition can be halted when the correct level of acidity has been obtained.

Excess acidity and de-acidification
Over acid wine is objectionable, and to render it drinkable the balance of acidity must of necessity be corrected by reducing the acid level. Several ways exist that can easily be used for achieving this objective.

(a) *Diluting to reduce acidity*
Before using this on a larger volume of wine, it should first be tried with a 500 ml (1 pint) sample.

It involves making a solution of sugar in boiled water to the same sweetness as that of the wine whose acidity is to be reduced. The sugar/water solution is added to the over acid wine with mixing until a taste sample shows the balance of acidity and sweetness to be satisfactory. If the flavour of a 500 ml sample is reduced to an unsatisfactory level as a result of using this dilution technique, either an alternative process must be used for the bulk or the flavour balance restored using one of the methods described later in this chapter.

(b) *Blending a high with a low acidity wine*

To use this method a wine of similar style but of low acidity has to be available in sufficient quantity. Because of this requirement, the method is rarely practical; however, where sufficient wine of low acidity exists, good results can be obtained.

All it entails is mixing some of the high acidity wine into that with low acidity until the acidity of the latter wine is considered to be at an acceptable level.

Low acidity wine should not be added to high acidity wine as this can result in all the low acid wine being used up and the resultant wine still having an unacceptably high acidity.

(c) *Calcium carbonate B.P.*

This substance is purified chalk and when it is added to wine the calcium combines with the acid to form a salt, at the same time, carbon dioxide gas is given off. In order to remove as much of the salt formed as possible, it is desirable to chill the treated wine and maintain it at a low temperature for several days, followed by racking and filtration.

Ideally the amount of acidity by which the wine is to be reduced should first be determined by taking a sample of the wine and measuring its acidity; then, using a second sample, cautiously adding very finely divided calcium carbonate, with stirring and tasting after each addition until about the right level of acidity is achieved and then measuring the level of acidity remaining. The amount of acidity to be removed can then be found easily by subtracting one value from the other viz:

% acidity to be removed = % acidity in wine before treatment minus % acidity in wine after treatment.

Measuring acidity

The method used for determination of Total Acidity is as follows:

Two chemicals are involved. One, a special dilution of caustic soda, or more correctly sodium hydroxide, which, as its name implies, is caustic, and if spilled and left on any painted or varnished surface, will remove the finish. Spillages should be cleaned up immediately, followed by a water rinse. Any contact with skin should be washed off with water. If upset on clothing, first wash out with water followed by water containing a little vinegar, then water again, as a final rinse.

The second chemical, phenolphthalein, is sometimes used as a purgative; it should not therefore come into contact with any food or drink for obvious reasons.

With simple precautions, these chemicals present no problem.

The other materials necessary for the test are a beaker which can be either glass or clear plastic, a graduated pipette, and a burette both preferably made of plastic since this will withstand accidental knocks much better than glass, and some distilled water which can be purchased from a chemist or a garage. Alternatively, the condensate around the coils of a refrigerator when it is defrosted can be used instead of distilled water.

Method for white wine

Into the beaker put about 100 mls of distilled water (this is just under 4 fl oz). Using the pipette measure 5 mls of wine and run this into the water, and add 5 drops of phenolphthalein indicator, swirl to mix.

Hold the burette in a stand or by means of a pair of Terry clips screwed to a board. Fill the burette to the 25 mls mark with N/10 sodium hydroxide, making sure the jet beneath the glass tap or clip is filled by allowing a little alkali to run out, and then topping up.

Run the N/10 sodium hydroxide into the wine a few drops at a time. keeping it swirling to mix. When the first pale pink appears stop, wait a moment, and if the colour remains note the burette reading, if not, add another drop. If the starting point was 25 mls on the burette, and after titration it is, say, 20.5 mls, then $25 - 20.5 = 4.5$ mls have been used, this volume is called the Titre. Titre $\times 0.15$ = Total Acidity as % tartaric acid in the wine.

Rose or red wines

The colour of wines interfere with the end point colour in the test above, and it is necessary to spot drops of indicator out on a white tile to have an external indicator. In other respects the test is virtually the same.

Procedure

Take a 100 mls quantity of distilled water in the beaker and add 5 mls of the wine, as described for a white wine.

Using a clean white tile (a spotting tile—one with little depressions—is ideal, but a flat white wall tile will do) put at intervals of 2″ or so 2 drops of phenolphthalein. Have about twelve lots spotted out.

Fill the burette with N/10 sodium hydroxide and add about 10 drops at a time with mixing, then with a glass rod remove a couple of drops, and mix with a spot of phenolphthalein. Keep adding and testing until a spot just turns pink. It may be necessary to rinse the tile and repeat the test, adding only 2 drops of alkali at a time between the point where the first pink colour was noticed and the previous colourless spot to obtain an accurate result.

The calculation is the same as for white wines.

Having found what percentage drop in acidity is necessary to balance the taste, it is a simple matter to calculate how much calcium carbonate is required for the volume of wine involved based on the assumption that 1 gm of calcium carbonate added to 1 litre of wine reduces the acidity, expressed as tartaric acid by 0.15%.

The quantity of calcium carbonate required for any known volume of wine can be calculated as follows:

$$\text{Volume of wine in litres} \times \frac{\% \text{ reduction in acidity required}}{0.15} = \text{gms of calcium carbonate necessary.}$$

Example of acid reduction calculation.

Say a wine had an acidity of 0.92% and after a trial de-acidification the acidity was 0.67 % and 4 litres of wine is to be adjusted.

The acidity reduction required is $0.92 - 0.67 = 0.25\%$.

Therefore: $4 \times \dfrac{0.25}{0.15} = 6.7$ gms of calcium carbonate is required.

The calcium carbonate can then be weighed out and dissolved in some of the wine, and then this wine added back with mixing into the bulk.

Wine which has been de-acidified in this manner should preferably be placed in a refrigerator (NOT a freezer) to reduce the solubility of the salts which will have been formed. After three to five days any insoluble salts will have come out of solution and be visible either as a deposit or a haze in the wine. Racking and filtration can then be performed to clarify it.

Care should always be taken to check that de-acidification has not reduced the pH below 3.5 as this will increase the risk of possible microbiological spoilage. A test with pH paper at the trial de-acidification stage will show if this is likely to be a problem.

(d) *Potassium carbonate*

Some winemakers advocate the use of this salt in preference to calcium carbonate, a view with which I do not agree. Potassium carbonate produces salts which are more soluble than those of calcium and consequently they remain in solution, even after refrigeration, as a result the pH is increased to a greater extent than when calcium carbonate is used. The taste can also be adversely affected.

(e) *Acidex for de-acidification*

Acidex is a proprietary product which comes from West Germany and basically is very finely divided calcium carbonate which is added to only part of the wine, the acidity of which is to be lowered to such an extent that the pH rises to 4.5 or greater. The result is a double salt of tartrate and malate is formed and this being particularly insoluble forms a deposit which can be filtered off. The treated wine is then blended back into the bulk of the wine, thereby reducing the overall acidity.

The method requires both malic and tartaric acids to be present for the double salt to be formed: it is therefore mainly applicable to wines made from fresh grape juice or grape concentrate. Other wines can be treated with Acidex but, without the combination of malic and tartaric acids, de-acidification takes place by formation of the simple calcium salts, viz., calcium malate, calcium citrate.

Method for using Acidex

First measure the acidity of the wine by either of the methods described earlier in this chapter then, using a separate sample of about 60 mls (2 fl oz), reduce the acidity by small additions of calcium carbonate until the taste is satisfactory. Next measure the acidity of the treated sample, and by subtracting one result from the other find the percentage decrease in acidity which is required viz: % acidity of wine— % acidity of de-acidified wine = % drop in acidity required.

The total volume of the wine has then to be measured in litres. Home winemakers sometimes find it more convenient to measure volumes in millilitres (or cc's); in this case the conversion to litres is a simple matter of dividing by 1000, viz: 3540 mls = 3.54 litres.

The weight of Acidex required is calculated in exactly the same way as that described for calcium carbonate, viz:

$$\frac{\text{Total volume of wine} \times \% \text{ drop in acidity required}}{0.15} = \text{gms of Acidex}$$

The volume of wine into which the Acidex has to be mixed to obtain a pH of 4.5 or greater has then to be calculated. For this the following formula is used:

$$\frac{1.05 \times \text{Wine volume in litres} \times \% \text{ drop in acidity required}}{\text{Acidity of untreated wine}}$$

= Litres of wine in which to dissolve Acidex

Example

3.54 litres of a wine with 0.92% acidity is to be de-acidified to 0.67% total acidity.

The weight of Acidex required is therefore:
$$\frac{3.54 \times (0.92 - 0.67)}{0.15} = 5.9 \text{ gms}$$
and the volume of wine to dissolve the Acidex:
$$\frac{1.05 \times 3.54 \times (0.92 - 0.67)}{0.92} = 1.01 \text{ litres (or 1010 mls)}$$

The procedure is to first dissolve the Acidex in about 1/10 of the calculated volume; for the example given this would mean using 100 mls from the 1010 mls.

Having dissolved the Acidex, the rest of the calculated volume (910 mls) is added with stirring to the wine containing Acidex (NOT Acidex treated wine into untreated wine).

After stirring for about 10 minutes this wine is then allowed to settle for 12–24 hours and then racked from the deposit formed followed by filtration. This wine will have been nearly neutralised—that is to say, its acidity will have dropped to a very low level—and this is then blended back into the untreated wine to give the acidity reduction orginally indicated by the simple calcium carbonate trial.

ASTRINGENCY

This is a term used to describe drying of the mouth caused by the presence of tannins (polyphenols). Excess astringency is not only undesirable, but also unpleasant to the taste and calls for the level to be reduced to a more acceptable point. An easy way of achieving this objective is fining with gelatine solution, and this procedure is described below.

Conversely, a lack of tannin can result in a wine lacking in zest, and it may therefore be necessary to increase the tannin level to get a satisfactory balance with the sweetness and acidity present.

Lack of tannin

A wine can be corrected for a lack of tannin by simply adding, with stirring and tasting, small quantities of tannic acid BP. Additions are stopped when the right flavour balance has been obtained.

It is recommended that only tannic acid of BP or an equivalent grade of purity be used for this purpose, as all the tannins in this material are hydrolysable, and therefore meet the EEC requirement for tannin added to beverages.

Excess tannin

Gelatine Fining is the best way of coping with this problem.

Procedure

Make a 1% solution of gelatine by dissolving 1 gm of gelatine BP in very hot water. Do not boil as this starts decomposition of the gelatine into other products by a process known as hydrolysis. Allow to cool. A fresh solution should be prepared for each trial.

Into each of six 125 ml clear glass bottles, measure 100 cc's of wine. Using a 5 mls graduated pipette—this can be purchased from a laboratory supplier—add 0.5, 1.0, 1.5, 2.0, 2.5 and 3.0 cc's of 1% gelatine to the jars respectively. Shake each jar and label it so that the next day it is clear which is which. On the following day examine the bottles and taste the contents of each. Look for the one giving the best tannin balance with the smallest gelatine addition. In this way you will not overfine.

For example, say 2.5 mls of 1% gelatine solution in 100 mls of wine gave excellent results: it is then possible to calculate the addition of gelatine necessary for the bulk of the wine.

The quantity of gelatine needed to fine the bulk of the wine is obtained from the best result of the fining trial, and calculated as follows:

$$\frac{\text{Total volume of wine in litres} \times \text{mls of 1\% gelatine for best result}}{10}$$

= gms gelatine.

The gelatine is then weighed out and dissolved in hot water, as previously, allowed to cool and then added with thorough mixing to the wine.

FLAVOUR AND WARMTH

The raw materials contribute to the flavour certain characteristics which enables an experienced winemaker to define what the basic predominating fruit juice or extract was. Sometimes a flavour is too strong, for instance, a raspberry wine can have such a strong aroma and taste that it is difficult to remember that it is a wine and not the juice of the fruit without any fermentation activity having occurred. Conversely, the amount of water used to extract fruits can be so overdone that the final wine is deficient in flavour.

Very full flavoured wines can be blended with wine of neutral or bland character to produce a diminished flavour yet possessing all the other desirable characteristics that were present in the two wines. This pre-supposes that well balanced wines of similar acidity and sweetness were blended together, or alternatively steps were taken to make them compatible by one or more of the processes described earlier in this chapter.

A strong flavoured wine, providing it is of an agreeable nature can be most useful. Small quantities of it can be blended into less strongly flavoured wines to produce a delicate character, whereas progressively greater amounts will improve the flavour style to an increasing extent.

The Elderberry wine, a recipe for which is given in Chapter 2, page 45, and the Raspberry wine described in Chapter 3, page 53, are excellent examples of red wines which are strong in flavour and therefore useful for blending purposes. Other wines can be prepared to have very strong flavour characteristics and used in a similar way. However, caution should be exercised not to overdo the extraction of the peel from citrus fruits, as some of their essential oils retard fermentation activity. This does not apply to the natural juice of the fruit but only to the peel.

It will be obvious from what has been said that flavour deficient wines can be boosted and improved by blending with wines of more flavoursome nature, but having said this, it has to be acknowledged that suitable wines for blending will not always be conveniently available. Under these circumstances it is possible to add flavouring. This subject has already been dealt with in Chapter 3, and the remarks made there concerning the use of flavourings to improve aroma apply equally well to taste improvement. A galaxy of flavouring compounds is now available for the winemaker, some seeking to impart the flavour obtained by oxidation in oak casks, whilst others seek to reproduce the flavour of Muscatel or Pedro Ximenez grapes used in the production of some commercial wines; Orange, Lemon, Lime, Grapefruit, Raspberry, and many more figure in the list of flavourings available. Each company manufacturing flavourings produces a different style to its competitors, some companies specialise in citrus fruits, whilst others go for the more exotic flavourings. Flavourings are also available as synthetic, that is to say, made by chemical synthesis techniques, and flavourings coming in this category, whilst conjuring up the flavour of a particular fruit or wine may not necessarily contain any of the compounds which go to give that particular flavour in the natural product. A second class of flavourings "Nature Identical" do consist of the same flavouring compounds found in the natural products, although the compounds themselves might have been manufactured in a factory or laboratory. The third classification is that of natural flavourings. These consist only of flavourings which have been extracted from natural products.

Synthetic flavourings have a habit of appearing to be exactly that, whilst by and large the other two classifications produce better overall impressions of the flavours they seek to recreate. This must not be taken as a statement of absolute fact but only as a guide, and the reader is recommended to experiment with small volumes of wine before treating a large volume with any flavouring material.

The overall flavour of a wine is a combination of very many factors, including sweetness, acidity, alcohol, the raw materials and the products of fermentation and maturation. Sometimes a boost in the apparent alcohol content is required so that a wine has a warm feel and aftertaste in the mouth. Within limitations this can be obtained by the judicious use of root ginger extract. This is sold as tincture or essence of ginger. Ginger flavouring is *not* the same thing. The reason for this is that ginger contains a resin—gingerene—and it is this which is extracted by alcohol to form the tincture or essence. A drop or two of the concentrated essence mixed into a bottle of wine will improve the warming effect it has on the palate, at the same time having little effect on the overall flavour, thereby creating an illusion of higher alcohol content than is in fact present. This is a very useful ploy when using wines for the preparation of "cups" or "punches". More than

71

two drops can, of course, be used if desired, but it is best to proceed a drop at a time, followed by tasting so that the dose is not overdone.

Much can therefore be done to improve the taste of a wine and at the same time derive enjoyment from achieving something which at first sight, might have appeared a lost cause.

CHAPTER 5

—PROTECTING THE WINE—

In general, wines should be protected from the extremes of temperature, both hot and cold, the effects of sunlight, oxidation and finally, microbial spoilage.

Protection from extremes of temperature

Wines exposed to the high temperatures sometimes experienced during English summers show more marked oxidation and change of colour to a browner shade than similar wines which have been stored in a cool cellar. The reason for this is the higher the temperature, the more quickly the chemical oxidation reactions proceed and it is therefore beneficial to store wines at an even temperature between 10°C and 15.5°C (50° to 60°F). Wines with higher alcohol content are more resistant to the effects of higher temperatures than light low alcohol table wines.

If a cellar affording good temperature control is not available, then the next best thing is to store wines during the summer months in a room of the house or outbuilding which receives the least direct sunlight, and has some natural ventilation even if this is only an open window. This is far preferable to leaving the wine in a room which receives a considerable amount of solar heat, so that, in effect, it receives a minor "cooking". If the latter situation is allowed to occur, the character of the wine is changed markedly, the bouquet is dulled, and in extreme cases takes on a Madeira wine aroma and the flavour loses its highlights and becomes dulled.

Exposure of wine to low temperature can have two effects: (i) a stabilising influence, the low temperature promoting the precipitation of nearly insoluble salts in the form of crystals, or (ii) a freezing of the wine with the effect that some of the water is converted to ice and the liquid remaining is consequently richer in alcohol and other dissolved solids.

In the first case, the salts precipitated are usually the potassium or calcium salts of tartaric acid, especially if grapes or grape concentrate has been used to make the wine. It is beneficial in this case to have the salts deposited and clear wine left which in the future, should it be exposed to lower temperature by for instance, placing a bottle of the wine in a refrigerator to cool it before serving, will remain stable and not throw a deposit of crystals when least expected. Formation of ice within the body of the wine might at first sight be attractive to the imbiber of higher alcohol wines, but it must be remembered that removing some of the water upsets the balance of the other dissolved solids remaining in the wine, and what was a very palatable wine before the freezing process might turn out to be a very unbalanced wine afterwards.

Sunlight

Sunlight consists to a large extent of ultra violet light, and this has the effect of speeding up the maturation of wine, whilst at the same time bleaching its colour. For this reason wines should be stored in a dark place, or failing this, in the shade away from direct sunlight.

Oxidation

This is the principal reaction that is speeded up by exposure to higher temperatures or direct sunlight.

When a new wine has been freshly fermented, it is largely free from oxygen or dissolved air because, during the course of the fermentation, carbon dioxide gas has been produced, and this in its turn has sparged out the air which may have been present over the surface of the wine, to create a protective blanket between the wine and the atmosphere. Similarly the, process of fermentation will have removed any dissolved oxygen from the wine itself. When wine is transferred by racking from the fermentation vessel to a fresh vessel for maturing, some addition of dissolved oxygen is inevitable, but the quantity can be contained by using the technique of transfer shown in Fig. 11. Even so, it is necessary to provide the wine with some additional protection at this stage and this is accomplished by adding sulphur dioxide in the form of sodium metabisulphite at a dose rate of 1 gm per 4.5 litres of wine. What happens is the sulphur dioxide reacts with any dissolved oxygen to bind it, and thereby minimises the effect it would have upon oxidation of the wine. This should be regarded as a must at the racking stage for all wines, white, red and rosé, sweet, medium dry or dry. In this way many disappointments will be avoided.

Preventing yeast or bacterial spoilage

All too easily, wines can be infected by either acid tolerant bacteria and/or yeasts. If the wine is not protected against these invaders, serious consequences will result, and more often than not the wine will be spoiled to such an extent that the winemaker in frustration uses it for cleaning the plumbing system of his or her house by flushing it down the drain. Fortunately this is the extreme situation, and steps can be taken quite easily to prevent such a happening occurring,

Broadly speaking, the winemaker has two options open: (i) to protect the wine from oxidation by the addition of a small dose of sulphur dioxide, then bottle the wine, securely cork it, and then expose the bottles to a temperature which will kill off any micro organisms which might be present, followed by cooling back to room temperature, or (ii) to incorporate into the wine a larger dose of sulphur dioxide, so that it not only acts as an anti-oxidant, but also is present at a sufficient level to be an anti-microbial agent also.

In the past great reliance has been placed on the second course of action by home winemakers because of the relative ease of adding a small amount of sodium metabisulphite powder to the wine before the bottling operation. However, the condition of the bottles and corks used during the bottling is vital to the success of this line of action, and it is not unknown for resistant strains of yeast to ferment in wine which has a relatively high quantity of sulphur dioxide present. One particularly widely occurring yeast called saccharomy-codes ludwigii has been found by the author to be growing in grape concentrate wine to which had been added 500 ppm of sulphur dioxide and this is about twice the quantity of sulphur dioxide normally found in commercial wines. Good hygiene practice is therefore essential and bottles must be not only cleaned thoroughly, but sterilised as well, and the same applies to the corks or caps going on to the bottles.

75

The acidity of the wine has a large bearing on how effective sulphur dioxide is in resisting micro-biological spoilage.

Effect of pH on sulphur dioxide

Wines should have their acidities adjusted so that the acid balance or pH is below 3.5. The reason for this is that sulphur dioxide is much more effective in preventing micro organism spoilage below this value than above it. There is no reason for thinking that this is a complicated test which the home winemaker cannot perform, an indicator paper is available and sold through most suppliers of wine making equipment which allows the winemaker to estimate the pH of his or her wine by simply tearing off a strip of the paper, dipping it into the wine and then comparing it with a standard colour scale which is supplied with the indicator paper. If the pH is too high the acidity of the wine must be adjusted by adding some acid to the wine, at the same time taking small samples and tasting to ensure that the acid balance is not unduly upset, and when the desired pH is obtained, no more acid need be added. There are occasions when a wine has a particularly high pH which needs to be brought down, but to do so by the addition of citric, tartaric or malic acid would involve adding so much acid as to make the wine unpalatable. Under these circumstances it is possible to add a few drops of ortho phosphoric acid which can be obtained from a laboratory supplier or a pharmacist. In which case, only food grade acid should be used.

OTHER METHODS OF PROTECTION

Potassium sorbate

The addition of sorbic acid, potassium sorbate or sodium sorbate is now widely practised in many winemaking regions to protect wines from possible yeast growth. Sorbic acid and its salts, whilst having anti-fungal activity, does not have any anti-bacterial properties. It is therefore not possible to omit sulphur dioxide and use potassium sorbate instead, because this would allow any spoilage bacteria present to gain a much better hold in the wine than would have been the case if some sulphur dioxide had been present since sulphur dioxide does have anti-bacterial properties.

76

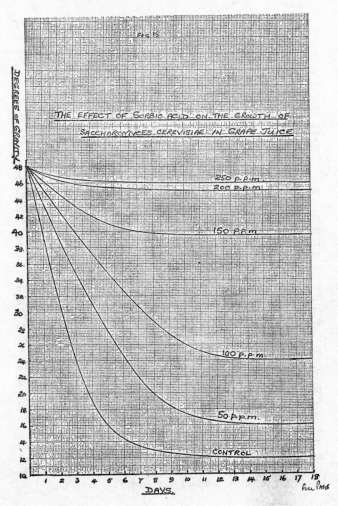

Fig. 15.

THE EFFECT OF SORBIC ACID ON THE GROWTH OF SACCHAROMYCES CEREVISIAE IN GRAPE JUICE

250 p.p.m.
200 p.p.m.
150 p.p.m.
100 p.p.m.
50 p.p.m.
CONTROL

DEGREES OF GRAVITY

DAYS.

Fig. 15.

77

The author has found potassium sorbate useful in preventing secondary fermentation in white wines containing some residual sugar, and has tested the effect of the preservative at different concentrations in a series of fermentations made from grape concentrate, each of which was sweetened to 48° of gravity, and saccharomyces yeast added to each at approximately the same dose level. The Fig. 15 shows the results which were obtained, and it will be seen that a concentration between 200 and 250 ppm gave the best result. This approximates to 1.5 gm of potassium sorbate per 4.5 litres of wine.

Potassium sorbate should not be used in any wine which has not been previously treated with sulphur dioxide to kill any bacteria which may be present, since it has been found that a geranium-like aroma and taste is sometimes produced in wines which have been treated with sorbates, and have subsequently been found to have contained lactic acid bacteria. It is believed that the bacteria produces a chemical* which then enters into combination with the sorbic acid to produce the geraniol aroma and flavour.

Off flavours have also been observed in red wines which have been treated with potassium sorbate, and it is possible that the reason for this is the same as for white wines which have not been treated with sulphur dioxide, because many winemakers believe that red wines do not require the addition of sulphur dioxide prior to bottling—this is a fallacy.

For those who do not have a simple balance with which to weigh out potassium sorbate powder, tablets containing potassium sorbate are available; these are manufactured by Southern Vinyards Ltd., Hove, Sussex, and can be obtained from many stockists of home winemaking equipment. On average, each tablet contains the equivalent of 630 mg of sorbic acid, therefore 1 tablet added to 4.5 litres effectively adds 140 ppm of sorbic acid, and as it is impractical to break tablets, 2 should be added to each 4.5 litres in order to obtain a quantity sufficient to retard yeast growth.

Benzoic acid

This preservative is commonly used in soft drinks, usually in
*Hexadienol Lactate

78

the form of the sodium or potassium salt, i.e. sodium or potassium benzoate. Its function is to inhibit the growth of yeast or moulds, and it has little or no effect on bacteria and does not function as an anti-oxidant. It is therefore similar in some ways to potassium sorbate. The effect of benzoic acid decreases with rise in pH, or put another way, the greatest effect is obtained in acidic liquids, and since wines fall into this category they provide a good medium. Unlike potassium sorbate, there is no risk of the formation of the geranium-like aroma or flavour but the effect on yeast and moulds is not so marked as that of sulphur dioxide, or, in the author's experience, as potassium sorbate.

Tablets of sodium benzoate are sold, and each tablet adds the equivalent of approximately 50 ppm of benzoic acid when added to 4.5 litres of wine.

It must be borne in mind that if this preservative is used, sodium metabisulphite or Campden tablets should also be added to give some sulphur dioxide, which will, in its turn, provide protection against possible bacterial attack and oxidation.

The winemaker therefore has at his or her disposal three chemical preservatives: (i) sulphur dioxide in the form of sodium metabisulphite or Campden tablets, which is effective against a mixed micro flora of yeast, moulds and bacteria, acts as an anti-oxidant, but is sensitve to pH, (ii) potassium sorbate, also available in tablets, but only effective against yeast and moulds, and (iii) sodium benzoate which is of limited effect against yeasts and moulds, is sensitive to pH. and can also be obtained in the form of tablets.

Heat as a preserving agent

It has already been said that some sulphur dioxide addition at the bottling stage is important to protect the wine from oxidation, but heat can be used for protection against microbiological spoilage from either yeast or bacteria.

The only practical way for the home winemaker to use heat for preserving his or her wine is to subject the bottles and contents after corking to sufficient heat to pasteurise the wine. This can be accomplished as follows:

1. First assemble the equipment which will be necessary;

a 0-100°C stirring thermometer, a bottle the same shape and size to that containing the wine, but filled with water and not corked, sufficient hot water and a deep sink or other large pan in which to place the bottles.

2. The sink or pan is filled about $\frac{1}{3}$ full with water, the temperature of which has been adjusted to about 70°C. Into this are placed the bottles of wine, with the bottle containing water with the thermometer in it, in the middle. The water temperature *in* the bottle is watched carefully, and the water in the sink or bowl adjusted to approximately 61°C by adding some hot water in small quantities in different places, not all in one spot. Keep the temperature steady and when the thermometer in the bottle reads 60°C, time 20 minutes and at the end of this period, remove the bottles from the hot water and cool them.

If properly carried out, this process will prevent secondary fermentation or bacterial spoilage of the wine.

Sugar/alcohol balance as a means of preventing secondary fermentation

For a long time it has been known that some sweet wines resist secondary fermentation better than others. A Russian scientist, Delle, put forward an equation which related the stability to sweetness and alcohol content in a given wine as follows :-

$$a + 4.5c = DU.$$

Where

a = The % of total sugar expressed as glucose in the wine
c = The % by volume of alcohol in the wine
DU = Delle Units (Units of Stability)

Delle found if DU exceeded 80, good stability usually existed. Since then, other workers have shown that stability varies, some wines being stable at 75 DU's whilst some require up to 85 DU's.

For home winemaking purposes the author has found 80 to be satisfactory.

It is possible for the winemaker to take advantage of this information only if the alcohol and sugar content of the wine to be stabilised can be measured. Both of these parameters can be approximately determined as follows:

(a) **Sugar content**

First take 10 mls of wine and boil it carefully in a test tube, making sure not to allow splashing out of the tube, for 10 minutes. After boiling, cool the tube and contents, and using water restore the volume to 10 mls.

For the next stage. 5 clean dry test tubes are required.

Into each of the tubes is first put 5 drops of boiled wine followed by water as shown below.

Tube	Drops of water	Dilution of original wine
1	5	2
2	10	3
3	20	5
4	30	7
5	40	9

The same dropper should be used for both boiled wine and the water, taking care to wash it thoroughly first.

The tubes are thoroughly mixed, and then tested as follows:

Sugar test

Apparatus required: 2 Pyrex glass test tubes; 1 bottle of Clinitest tablets for estimating sugar in urine; 1 Clinitest dropper. All available from Pharmacists.

Clinitest tablets are manufactured by Ames Company, Slough, who supply with each bottle of tablets a colour comparison chart for use in urine testing; it is this which is used for this test on wine.

Method

Make sure both test tubes are clean and dry.

Rinse out the dropper with clean water and flick out any surplus by shaking quickly in a downwards direction.

Suck up some of the diluted wine from the first tube of boiled and diluted wine, and place 5 drops in a test tube. Expel any excess in the dropper, and carefully wash it out with running water, then add 10 drops of water to the same tube. Gently agitate the tube to thoroughly mix the contents.

Into the second tube place 15 drops of water only.

Into both tubes add a Clinitest tablet. Wait for the bubbling to cease, and then after 15 seconds, shake the tubes gently and

81

compare them with the colour chart. The tube containing water only should give a blue negative (zero percent sugar) colour.

If the colour indication for the wine is that of $\frac{1}{4}\%$, the next tube in the series—the one with a dilution factor of 3 should give a similar result, and it will therefore be necessary to repeat the test using *undiluted* wine that has been boiled and cooled. Similarly, if an indication greater than 2% is shown by the fifth tube in the dilution series (representing a 9-fold dilution of wine) a second series of tubes will need to be prepared at double the dilutions shown, ie, 10, 20, 40, 60 and 80 drops of water to 5 drops of wine in order to obtain two results which can be bracketed together as shown in the example.

Observe the colour of each tube immediately the chemical reaction ceases, and compare immediately with the colour chart supplied with the tablets.

Example

If tube 4 gave an indication of 1% and tube 5 was $\frac{3}{4}\%$, the wine would contain between $1\% \times 7$ (the dilution of the original wine in tube 4)$=7\%$ and $\frac{3}{4}\% \times 9$ (the dilution of the original wine in tube 5)$= 6.75\%$. An average value of 6.88% can be taken, and 6.9% is a near enough approximation.

Note: it is important to "bracket" the sugar content between 2 colours at two dilutions to get a reasonable approximation.

(b) Alcohol content

The following method is adapted from that described by Dr. W. Honneyman..

First measure the specific gravity of the wine as accurately as possible, using a hydrometer with a scale divided at one degree intervals.

The specific gravity needs to be determined with a hydrometer at least 20 cms in length, to have any chance of reading the scale with a reasonable degree of accuracy. This rules out the use of combination sampling/specific gravity devices (Fig. 17) constructed along the lines of car battery testers which will go through the neck of a 4.5 litre fermentation jar. The hydrometer in this case is too small for the purpose. The reader is also reminded that it is important to read the scale of the hydrometer, when it is floating in the wine at eye level to eliminate what is known as parallax (see Fig. 16).

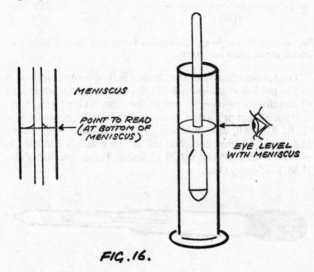

MENISCUS

POINT TO READ
(AT BOTTOM OF
MENISCUS)

EYE LEVEL
WITH MENISCUS

FIG. 16.

Measure out 200 mls of the wine to be tested using a measuring cylinder, or better still a volumetric flask of 200 mls capacity.

Transfer the wine into a saucepan and wash out the flask or cylinder with about 20 mls of water and add this to the saucepan. Gently simmer until the volume is reduced to a little more than $\frac{1}{3}$ the original volume.

Taking care not to allow water into the saucepan, cool the contents to 20°C and then transfer them back into the measuring cylinder or flask and restore the volume to 200 mls by adding water, and thoroughly mix. Finally measure the specific gravity using the same hydrometer as that used for the original specific gravity of the wine.

The alcohol content can then be calculated as follows:

Specific gravity of the dealcoholised and volume restored

83

wine minus the Specific gravity of the original wine=The spirit indication. Then,

$$\frac{1000-(\text{Spirit indication}+0.16^*)}{1000} = \begin{array}{l}\text{Approximate specific}\\ \text{gravity of alcohol in the}\\ \text{wine}\end{array}$$

*0.16 is Dr. Honneyman's correction factor and should always be added to the spirit indication.

The specific gravity of the alcohol is then looked up in one of the published tables to find the corresponding percentage of alcohol by volume present in the wine. Table 1 is a modification of that printed in *Scientific Winemaking—made easy* (J. R. Mitchell, also published by the Amateur Winemaker Ltd.) and for more complete tables, the reader's attention is drawn to the Official 20/20°C Spirit Tables published by H.M. Stationery Office.

FIG. 17.

TABLE 1

Degrees, British proof spirit	% Alcohol by volume	Specific gravity of alcohol
10	5.8	0.9918
11	6.3	0.9911
12	6.9	0.9903
13	7.5	0.9846
14	8.1	0.9888
15	8.6	0.9882
16	9.2	0.9875
17	9.8	0.9867
18	10.3	0.9861
19	10.9	0.9854
20	11.5	0.9847
21	12.1	0.9840
22	12.7	0.9833
23	13.2	0.9827
24	13.8	0.9821
25	14.4	0.9814
26	14.9	0.9809
27	15.5	0.9802
28	16.1	0.9795
29	16.7	0.9789
30	17.2	0.9784
31	17.8	0.9777
32	18.4	0.9771
33	19.0	0.9764
34	19.5	0.9759
35	20.1	0.9752

The above table is approximate in the fourth decimal place for alcohol specific gravity and correct to one place of decimals for the comparison of Degrees British Proof Spirit and % alcohol by volume.

Example

A wine is found to have a specific gravity of 1.011 and the sugar test showed approximately 6.9% of sugar present.

The alcohol test was performed and the liquid in the pan after simmering and restoring the volume to 200 mls was found to have a specific gravity of 1.028.

Calculations:

The spirit indication is therefore $1.028 - 1.011 = 17$.

Then the Specific Gravity of the alcohol in the wine is;

$$\frac{1000 - (17 + 0.16)}{1000} = \frac{982.84}{1000} = 0.9828$$

From Table 1. 0.9827 equals 13.2% v/v alcohol.

Then the Delle stability number is $6.9 + (4.5 \times 13.2) = 66.3$

Conclusion

Assuming 80 DU's to be necessary for stability, this wine cannot be considered stable, and it might secondary ferment.

Using fortification to improve stability

A reasonably easy calculation can be made on the basis of the Delle equation to calculate how much alcohol is necessary to achieve stability.

Example

80 DU's are required for stability.

The wine has been calculated to have 66 DU's (omitting the 0.3 for easy calculation). Therefore a further $80 - 66 = 14$ DU's are required.

As each 1% v/v of alcohol contributes 4.5 DU's, if the alcohol content of the wine is raised by $14/4.5 = 3.1$% v/v the wine would be stable.

Source of alcohol for fortification

Vodka is the most easily obtained neutral spirit suitable for fortification, and it is sold at 37.5, 40, 48.6 and 51.5% by volume alcohol strengths. The two higher strengths being the best to use if obtainable.

Say the 13.2% v/v alcohol wine was to be raised by 3.1% v/v to 16.3% v/v using 40% v/v vodka. The calculation is very simple, using the St. Andrews Square Calculation technique.

First draw a St. Andrews Cross.

Simply write the existing wine strength (13.2% v/v) at the top left, and the vodka strength (40% v/v) at the top right.

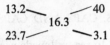

The desired alcoholic strength (16.3% v/v) is written in the middle.

Each of the top values is taken from the centre value and the result written at the other end of the cross arm, i.e. $16.3 - 13.2 = 3.1$. This is written on the same cross arm but at the other end to that with 13.2, as shown above.

The calculation shows 23.7 litres of wine at 13.2% v/v alcohol plus 3.1 litres of vodka at 40% v/v will give $23.7 + 3.1 = 26.8$ litres of wine at 16.3% v/v which will be stable. If only 1 litre of wine is to be stabilised by fortification use $3.1/23.7 = 0.131$ litres (or 131 mls of Vodka).

There is nothing complicated about the calculation, it is in fact much easier than finding out if you have the Tote Double at Ascot!

CHAPTER 6

BOTTLES, CORKS, CAPS AND CAPSULES

It is not uncommon to see well-made wine presented either in the wrong colour bottle, or badly capped or corked. The secret of success is for the winemaker to have on hand not only bottles which will enhance and protect the wine, but also closures which will fit the bottles properly. Finally the overall appearance of the package can be greatly enhanced by the application of a capsule over the closure, and in a suitably contrasting colour to give the bottled wine immediate eye appeal.

Bottles

Bottles fulfil two basic functions. Firstly they provide a means of containing the wine in suitable size quantities depending upon the volume of the bottles used for use at table or in other circumstances as the occasion demands, and secondly, if the bottle is suitably coloured, provide protection against the effects of light.

White and rosé wines are traditionally packed in clear glass bottles, and are therefore afforded no protection by the colour of the glass acting as a light filter. If a wine has artificial colour added to it or has been prepared by the addition of a colouring wine such as beetroot or elderberry, as described in an earlier chapter to produce a delicate pink or red tinge, it is better to bottle the wine in a light brown bottle. Red wines should always be bottled into either brown or dark green bottles. The reason for this is that brown or dark green coloured glass filters out that part of the light spectrum which has the greatest effect upon the colour of a wine, brown glass is a more effective filter than green, and dark brown glass offers better protection than the light brown. It therefore makes good sense to store wines in bottles of a colour which will protect them and preserve the colour up to the actual time of drinking.

It is, of course, a mistake not to show off the colour of a wine when serving it, or showing it at a wine show or exhibition. As was said earlier, beetroot wine suffers from the effects of light, and therefore needs to be kept not only in a dark bottle, but in a dark place to preserve its colour and prevent it changing to a mahogany brown shade. However, if a particularly good beetroot wine is going to be exhibited, it would be sensible, just before departing for the event, to decant the wine carefully into a clear glass bottle, cap or cork it, dress it with a capsule and label it so that it is displayed on the stand with its colour for all to see. Likewise, if serving such a wine at table, it should be decanted into a clear glass carafe or decanter so that the diners can appreciate the skill that the winemaker has shown in preserving the colour for their enjoyment.

The choice of bottle shape rests with the winemaker, but it is true to say that red wines intended for table use look best in either a burgundy or claret shaped dark bottle, whilst dessert wines take their rightful place on the sideboard when packaged in one of the familiar fortified wine bottle shapes such as the traditional London bottle either with a cork or a screw cap.

Caps

Over the last 10 years, there has been something of a revolution away from the traditional corks towards polythene stoppers and caps, as well as metal caps fitted with a seal suitable for contact with wine.

The polythene type stopper offers many attractions for the home winemaker, for one thing, it can be re-used, and does not require the insertion of a corkscrew with consequent damage to remove it. It is also easier to use than cork, and does not suffer from the same problems that corks do of having numerous air passages which can harbour mould spores or even bacteria and yeast which can either destroy the flavour of a wine, or if the corks have not been properly prepared, start micro-biological spoilage. However, there are disadvantages as well, polythene does not "breathe", that is to say, it does not allow the passage of air that cork does, and in this way, it prevents diffusion of air into the wine which some people consider necessary for good maturation, particularly for red wines. Also, whilst cork can be made to conform to irregular shapes in the necks of bottles, the same is not true of polythene. If a good seal is to be obtained, then the bottle must be a good fit to the closure and it cannot be over-emphasised that if this is not checked and bottles are placed on their side leakage will most probably occur.

Polythene caps of the screw pattern should be checked against the bottle on which they are to be fitted to ensure that the threads are complementary. It is also important to check that the cap contains a pad or wad as it is sometimes called, in the top which is suitable for contact with wine. Metal faced wads should be avoided unless it is certain that the shiny surface of the metal is covered with melamine or some other approved coating for contact with wine or acidic foods. Because of its acidity wine readily attacks metal and if an aluminium surface is exposed to the wine, some of that metal will be dissolved and eventually a haze or deposit will appear in the wine. Under no circumstances should metal caps with only a lacquer coating be used in contact with wine. It cannot be too strongly emphasised that because of its acidic nature, wine will dissolve metals and this means that if the protection afforded between the wine and the metal surface is so thin that the wine can penetrate it, even through minute pinholes which might exist in the lacquer finish, eventually gross attack of the base metal will take place and if that metal contains heavy metal impurities, consumption of the wine could be injurious to health.

Corks

If the choice of corks has been made, then the winemaker's attention is drawn to considering which length is most suitable for the bottling to be carried out. Short corks are more suitable for wine which is to be stored for a relatively short period of time, that is to say, 6–18 months, whereas, the longer corks, are more suitable for wines which are to be stored for maturation over a period of several years. The author recommends the 3.2 to 3.8 cm length cork for white wines in particular, since these are usually consumed while still young, but for elderberry, which requires at least five

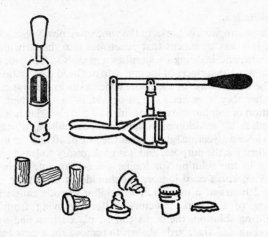

FIG. 18.

The illustration shows two different corking tools, one an all-metal device, and the other made of wood. On the left is a selection of corks with the finest straight grain through to the coarsest type, whilst in the foreground is a stopper cork and two different polythene stoppers along with a metal screw cap with its "wad".

years' storage to attain its best quality, the long 4.5 to 5cm cork is recommended.

When selecting corks, it is important to buy those which have a regular grain and few surface imperfections; many surface imperfections serving to indicate that the unseen structure of the cork is probably of a similar nature. The better the quality of the cork the less likelihood there is of wine seepage. The next thing to look for is that the corks have a slight spongy or springy feel, and are not hard and unyielding. Hard corks, by and large, shrink more than those which have a springy feel. The springy resilience is produced by air entrained in the natural structure of the cork and if air is present, then microbes might also be present. It is therefore essential to sterilise all corks before they are brought in contact with wine.

Sterilisation

Large suppliers of corks to the wine trade now subject them to a hot wax treatment that penetrates into the structure of the cork, and in doing so, sterilises and seals it. This does not mean that the surfaces of the corks do not need sterilisation.

The easiest way for the home winemaker to sterilise corks, whether they have been waxed or not, is to soak them in a solution of sulphur dioxide to which a little glycerine has been added. A 1% solution of sodium metabisulphite to which has been added glycerine (glycerol) at the rate of 10 mls per litre is excellent for the purpose, and it is unnecessary to leave waxed corks in the solution for longer than 30 minutes, whereas unwaxed corks need longer, but should not be left for more than 2 hours at a maximum as sulphur dioxide causes hardening of the cork structure. After removing from the sterilising solution, the corks can be placed in a fine nylon mesh bag and vigorously shaken to remove the excess before using them to cork bottles. A little sulphur dioxide solution will inevitably be squeezed from the cork when it is inserted in the bottle. It is most unlikely that this will result in any problems; in fact, the contrary is more likely to be the case, with the small amount of additional sulphur dioxide providing added resistance to oxidation.

It is a wise precaution to wash off polythene stoppers in a 1% solution of sodium metabisulphite before they are used to ensure that the surfaces have been effectively sterilised.

Under no circumstances should corks be placed into boiling water and boiled in an attempt to sterilise them, as this will inevitably result in hardening and subsequent brittleness, making not only corking more difficult, but also cork removal when the time comes. Corks which have been subjected to boiling water treatment frequently break up when a corkscrew is inserted.

The tool used to insert the cork into the bottle can be of either metal or wooden construction. However, if a wooden tool is used, care is necessary before each use to ensure that it is clean and does not have any residues of wine left on it which may have allowed the growth of spoilage micro-organisms. An effective way of making sure that a wooden corker is suitable for use, is to first of all thoroughly wash it and then dip it into a 1 % solution of sodium metabisulphite and leave it for 5–10 minutes before use, the steralent will by this time have soaked into the wood sufficiently to prevent the growth of undesirable microbes.

Capsules

There are now available on the market, attractive aluminium foil capsules in a range of colours which can be selected according to the colour of the bottle or the wine, to give a balanced attractive appearance when placed over the cap, cork or closure, and crimped on using a special tool. The capsules come preformed and only need to be placed over the closure and then rolled into place. Fig. 19 shows the kind of tool which is used for the crimping operation, along with a cut-away section to show how it operates. Essentially, a rubber ring is rolled over the surface of the capsule, crimping it close to the body of the bottle and the contours of the closure.

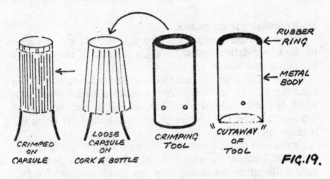

CRIMPED ON CAPSULE   LOOSE CAPSULE ON CORK & BOTTLE   CRIMPING TOOL   "CUTAWAY" OF TOOL   RUBBER RING   METAL BODY

FIG. 19.

It is still possible to obtain lead capsules and treat them in the same way, but whilst lead conforms easily to the contours of a bottle, it must be pointed out that lead produces poisonous salts with acids, and it is therefore necessary to make sure when removing a lead capsule from a bottle that the top of the neck surface is cleaned so that when the cork is removed the wine pours over a clean glass surface, not one which is possibly contaminated with lead salt.

Plastic capsules are also available.

93

CHAPTER 7

TURNING DISASTER INTO SUCCESS

All winemakers at some time or another, come across a situation where the wine either does not ferment properly and more residual sugar than was intended is left behind, making the wine sweet and completely out of balance, or alternatively have found when looking at wines in storage, that one of them has developed characteristics making it undrinkable. Both of these situations can be dealt with in a manner which will allow recovery of most of the wine. In the latter case, the remedy calls for extreme measures, hence the title of this chapter.

High remaining sugar content

This condition is usually due to the premature conclusion of the fermentation and there are a number of reasons why this sometimes occurs.

1. The acidity of the juice before fermentation may have been rather high, so that when more acids were formed as a result of the fermentation process, the pH or acid balance of the wine became too low for yeast growth, low pH being the result of high acidity.

To check if this is the cause of fermentation arrest is usually very easy, because the wine will taste sharp, although to some extent this might be masked by the sweetness, and for this reason it is always best to check the pH and acidity by the use of pH paper and the titration method. The pH is very easy to determine (see Chapter 5, p. 76), and gives an answer equally easy to understand. If the pH is shown to be too low—below pH 3.0—the wine will require diluting with boiled and cooled water to increase the pH to above 3.0, followed by the addition of a vigorous starter yeast culture together with a little yeast food (diammonium hydrogen phosphate). Alternatively the total acidity of the wine can be measured by titration (see Chapter 4, pp. 64–65) and if the acidity is greater than 1 %

expressed as citric acid (10 parts per 1000) the wine needs dilution with boiled and cooled water along with yeast food as described above.

In either case, provided warm storage conditions, fermentation usually then goes to completion. Finally the wine can be racked, fined and filtered as previously described, and any other corrective measures taken which may be thought necessary to improve the appearance, aroma or taste.

2. Sometimes the problem is due simply to excessive sugar having been added prior to fermentation. The maximum amount of sugar which most normal yeast will ferment is a concentration of approximately 1.35 kilos (about 3 lb) in 4.5 litres (1 gallon), above this concentration the osmotic pressure is too high for the yeast to function. The amount of sugar remaining can be checked by the use of a hydrometer, and if this shows the specific gravity to be higher than 1.110 the answer is once again to dilute with boiled and cooled water and reduce the specific gravity, and therefore the sugar concentration. A vigorous yeast culture then needs to be added, and the fermentation kept warm whilst it completes.

3. It is possible for a wine not to ferment out simply because there is insufficient nutrient material for the yeast to survive and the number of cells dying gradually exceeds the number of new cells being produced until finally fermentation stops. This situation is not uncommon in wines made from flower petals or where the juice of a fruit has been over-extended by the addition of sugar and water. Wines made from a rich fruit juice base rarely suffer in this way. If a wine therefore fails to complete its fermentation, but is in the right acid zone and does not have an excessive amount of sugar present, it is likely that lack of nutrient for the yeast to continue the fermentation process is the cause. The remedy is to add 3 gm of ammonium phosphate (diammonium hydrogen phosphate) to each 4.5 litres of wine together with half a gramme of so called yeast energiser, to the same volume. Yeast energiser is a mixture of amino acids and vitamins essential for the changes carried out by the yeast cells. Once again, a vigorous yeast culture then needs to be added and the fermentation kept warm.

The conditions just described are relatively minor compared

95

with the situation of a wine which has darkened and taken on a tired oxidised aroma and taste, or a red wine which has become harsh and somewhat acidic. To use such wines without any form of treatment is almost a guarantee of dissatisfaction with the final product, even if masking flavourings are added. Some off flavours are impossible to remove completely, whilst others respond readily to treatment. The most universal treatment consists of adding high quality activated carbon, often described as activated bone charcoal. This is finely ground carbon which has been subjected to heat treatment to make the surface area very adsorptive. What this means is that the enormous surface area of a comparatively small amount of carbon will take on to it chemicals giving rise to flavour and aroma by a physical process known as adsorption. This must not be confused with absorption, the one being an attachment to the surface by a physical process and the other a soaking into the matrices of the media, also a physical process, but one involving capilliary action. A wine subjected to carbon treatment will therefore have much of its colour, flavour and aroma stripped from it if a high enough dose of carbon is used. This takes place quite quickly after the carbon has been added, but because the carbon is so finely divided it takes 2–3 days to settle. When this has taken place, the wine can be carefully racked off from the carbon and fine filtered to give a near-neutral base into which can be added flavourings and colouring to produce a Vermouth or aperitif wine.

The range of herbs used to make such wines is very large, different mixtures being used to produce spicy, piquant, sweet, or bitter characteristics. Just a few of the herbs used are thyme, muscatel sage, calamus, Roman wormwood, peppermint, angelica, coriander, clove. Many more plants are used and the selection of which herbs to use for a particular Vermouth or aperitif requires great skill and knowledge, and is a closely guarded secret in the great commercial companies manufacturing such products with familiar names such as Martini, Nouilly Prat, Cinzano and Campari. Several suppliers have put together packets of herbs suitable for the preparation of different types of Vermouth, and these can be obtained from Ritchie Products, Burton-on-Trent, Staffs.,

Semplex Home Brews Ltd., Birkenhead, and many other suppliers. Ready made essences are also available.

How therefore, can this information be put into practice?

First of all the volume of the inferior wine is measured, and its specific gravity. If the wine is sweet then the choice of vermouth which can be made from it is limited, but if it is dry, either a dry, semi-sweet or sweet vermouth can be prepared. It is unlikely that the herbs or flavouring extract suitable for a sweet vermouth will also be suitable for a dry product, therefore the decision of what style vermouth is to be made has to be taken before the herbs or flavouring are purchased.

Next, to each 4.5 litres (1 gallon) of wine is added 15 gms (approx. $\frac{1}{2}$ oz.) of decolourising carbon followed by thorough mixing. The vessel containing the wine can then be corked and set aside for the carbon to settle.

Racking the wine from the carbon needs delicate handling; removing the cork or bung and inserting the syphon tube can stir up the deposit. It is best to fit the syphon tube to a suitable filter before putting it into the wine, as this will not only minimise possible agitation, but also allow the wine to be filtered bright at the same time as it is racked from the carbon lees. Either the homemade filter or one of the commercially available sheet filters which work on a gravity principle can be recommended for this purpose, and both are described in Chapter 2.

The wine, after clarification will have lost most or all of its colour, along with much of its aroma and flavour. In the case of red wines the depth of colour will be greatly reduced to possibly pale pink. This is just the right media into which can be added strong herbal flavours. Recork the wine and set it aside whilst the herbal extract is prepared.

Liquid herbal extracts can be purchased from most wine making suppliers, and come in a sufficiently wide range to accommodate most tastes. French and Italian styles are available both for sweet and dry wines. Making a semi-sweet product simply involves using a sweet vermouth extract but reducing the sugar addition.

For the more ambitious with a bit of the "I did it my way" spirit, packets of herbs are available and the names of two suppliers are given earlier in this chapter. The technique is to put the herbs into a suitably sized muslin or cotton bag which has been well washed, then insert this into a wide mouthed jar with just a little spare space above the bag; on to this is then poured a miniature bottle (50 mls) of Vodka. The jar is then topped up with some of the carbon treated wine. During the next two days the jar with the herbs and spirit needs to be shaken from time to time.

On the third day the extract will be ready for addition to the wine.

Before adding the herbal extract, add any sugar which may be necessary. A dry wine which is going to be made into a sweet vermouth will require quite a lot, and this can be added either to taste, that is to say stirring in sugar and tasting at intervals during the addition, and stopping when the taste is judged correct, or by the predetermined specific gravity method. If the latter method is used the specific gravity of the vermouth to be made has first to be decided, and then sugar is added until the hydrometer shows the predetermined reading. When using this technique a specific gravity of 1.038 is a good average for sweet vermouth, and 1.010 for semi-sweet.

Similarly the acidity of the wine should be adjusted, and this is best done by the addition and tasting method using citric acid made into a concentrated solution with a little of the wine, and adding this in small amounts to the bulk until the desired acidity is achieved.

Everything is then ready for the addition of the herbal extract. This is a very critical point in the whole operation and can ruin everything. For this reason, divide the wine into two equal volumes and then the herbal extract is added with a dropper a little at a time to one half only. If a mistake is made by adding too much extract the other half of the wine is available to dilute it to a satisfactory level. Having got one half right, the other can be treated. Two Campden tablets or 1 gm of sodium metabisulphite should then be added to each 4.5 litres of the vermouth to protect it from oxidation changes.

If a red vermouth is required and the wine is pale or white, either blend in a little deep coloured red wine or use a little of the Amaranth (E123), Cochineal (E120), Beetroot Red

(E162) or Enocyanin (E163) colouring described in Chapter 2.

Finally the vermouth (or bitters) is set aside to "marry" and mature for 1–2 months. It is then ready for drinking and goes very well with ice and lemon for cool summer drinks. Vermouths do not improve with keeping, the herbal flavours altering in character and diminishing in perceptibility with time, and as a result, the freshness of the aroma and flavour is lost.

CHAPTER 8

Useful Equipment and Materials

This Chapter has been compiled with the intention of providing the reader with a ready means of reference to the chemicals and apparatus referred to in the rest of the text.

Many of the items will be readily available from local stockists of amateur winemaker requisites but some pieces of equipment are best purchased from a laboratory supplier. It is best to select equipment in person at the supplier's premises. There will, however, be occasions when this is impractical and a list of selected suppliers of specialist laboratory apparatus is given.

Chemicals

Acidex—Manufactured by: C. H. Boehringer Sohn, 6507 Ingelheim Am Rhein, West Germany. U.K. Supplier: A. Massel & Co. Ltd., Weare Street, Ockley, Surrey.

Amaranth (E123 Colouring)

Ammonium phosphate (Diammonium hydrogen phosphate)

Ammonium sulphate

Amylase enzyme

Beetroot Red (E162 Colouring)

Bentonite

Calcium carbonate

Citric acid (Monohydrate)

Clinitest Tablets—Manufactured by: Ames Company, Slough, U.K., and available from Pharmacists

Cochineal (E120 Colouring)

Concentrated fruit juices

Decolorising bone carbon

Dried skimmed milk

Enocyanin (E163 Colouring)

Fructose

Flavourings

Glycerol (Glycerine)

Granulated sugar (Sucrose)

Herbs
Honey
Iodine solution
Isinglass
Lactic acid (50% solution)
Malic acid
Methylated spirit
Orthophosphoric acid
Pectinase enzyme
Phenolphthalein
Polyvinylpolypyrrolidone (PVPP)
Potassium carbonate
Potassium sorbate (available in tablet and powder form)
Root ginger extract
Sodium benzoate (available in tablet and powder form)
Sodium hydroxide N/10 strength
Sodium metabisulphite (available as Campden tablets as
    well as powder)
Sulfidex—U.K. Supplier: A. Massel & Co. Ltd., address as
    above.
Tannic acid B.P.
Tartaric acid
Tartrazine (E102 Colouring)
Vodka
Yeast—Dried etc.
Yeast energiser

Equipment
Buchner filter assembly—flask, funnel etc.
Burette
Capsule applicator
Capsules
Corks
Corker
Cotton wool
Fermentation jars 4.5 litre (1 gallon)
Filter funnels (large and small)
Filter paper
Filter pump
Filter media (Cellulose, Kieselguhr)

101

Filters of proprietary manufacturers (see text)
Graduated pipette (5 ml)
Hydrometer
Jar or cylinder for hydrometer
Liquidiser
Medicine bottles (50 mls)
Medicine spoon (5 mls)
Muslin
Nylon bag
pH papers
Plastic tubing
Polythene stoppers
Saucepan
Spotting Tile
Syphon or Racking tube
Table lamp
Tasting glasses
Test tubes
Thermometer
Volumetric flask (200 mls)
Wine bottles

Large Suppliers

General Laboratory Glassware and Equipment
Laboratory and Scientific Export Co. Ltd.,
Airfleet House, Sulivan Road, London SW6 3EP.
Baird & Tatlock (London) Ltd.,
PO Box 1, Romford, Essex RM1 1HA.
A. Gallenkamp & Co. Ltd.,
PO Box 290, Technico House, Christopher Street, London
EC2P 2ER.
Science Services Gmbh,
Frigda Strasse. 1. 8 Munchen, 8000, West Germany.

Specialist Suppliers of Plastic Apparatus
Azlon Products Ltd.,
Glyn Street, London SE11 5JG.
Nalgene Labware Dept.,
Nalge Co., PO Box 365, Rochester, New York, USA.
Science Services Gmbh,
Address as above.

Filter Media Suppliers
Whatman Ltd.,
Springfield Mill, Maidstone, Kent.
Whatman Inc.,
9 Bridewell Place, Clifton, New Jersey, 07014 USA.
Science Services Gmbh,
Address as above.

Chemicals and pH paper
BDH Chemicals Ltd.,
Poole, Dorset. BH12 4NN.
Hopkin and Williams,
PO Box 1, Romford, Essex RM1 1HA.
Fiske Assoc. Inc.,
Route 146, Uxbridge, Massachusetts, 01569 USA.
Pierce Eurochemie,
PO Box 1151, Rotterdam, Netherlands.
Science Services Gmbh.
Address as above.

Throughout this book reference has been made to the metric system of measuring both weights and volumes. Volume measurements are comparatively easy, as most kitchen measures are calibrated in both the metric and imperial (or United States') systems. Weights are, however, not quite so simple particularly where small quantities are involved. Comparatively cheap small scales can be purchased but for those readers who might like to make a simple balance, the following may be of interest.

Making a simple balance
If a simple balance is not available one can easily be made from 2 tin lids, 2 knitting needles, some thin twine, a medicine bottle and some sticky paper.

Technique of making balance

Hole

Take a round cork of approximately 12.5 mm diameter and 2.5 cms long and a plastic knitting needle of 10 gauge.

Fig 20

103

Drill a hole slightly smaller than the needle, in the middle of the cork.

Push the needle through the hole so that the cork is about central. Cut off the head of the needle with a hack saw, file the needle into a slight point and check the cork is central.

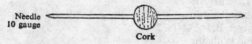

Needle
10 gauge

Cork

Fig. 21

Next take two small corks 9.5 mm diameter and 16 mm long approximately, and fit one to each end of the needle.

Fig 22

Now take a very fine knitting needle and trim it with a hack saw or tin snips so that it is 2.5 cms shorter than the medicine bottle height. Push this needle firmly into the middle cork so that it is central but at right angles to the 10 gauge needle.

Insert the fine needle into the bottle so that the large cork sits on the neck.

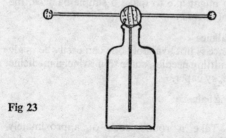

Fig 23

Using two tin lids of the same size (7.5 cms in diameter is ideal), mark a cross on the bottom of each with a pencil and punch a small hole in the rim above each of the cross ends

Fig 24

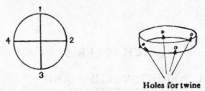

Holes for twine

Take four 23 cm lengths of twine and knot one end of each. Use a piece to join holes 1 and 2, and another to join holes 3 and 4. Tie the ends so that both loops on each lid are the same size.

Now suspend the pans one on each of the small corks.

The balance should now rest level and the fine knitting needle should be perpendicular. If this is not so and the balance goes down to the left, slide the left hand cork and pan in slightly towards the middle so that balance is obtained. If this is ineffective a little melted candle wax can be added to whichever pan is light.

All that then remains is to stick a strip of adhesive paper on the outside of the bottle and mark the balance point of the needle on it.

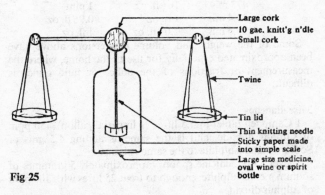

Large cork
10 gae. knitt'g n'dle
Small cork
Twine
Tin lid
Thin knitting needle
Sticky paper made into simple scale
Large size medicine, oval wine or spirit bottle

Fig 25

To enable weighings of $\frac{1}{4}$, $\frac{1}{2}$, $\frac{3}{4}$, 1, 2, 4, 6, 8 and 10 gm quantities, only a $\frac{1}{4}$, (0.25), $\frac{1}{2}$ (0.5), 1 gm, 2×2 gm and a 5 gm weight need be purchased.

CHAPTER 9

USEFUL WEIGHT, VOLUME AND TEMPERATURE CONVERSIONS—

	Metric	*Imperial*	*U.S.A.*
Weights	1 kilo	2.204 lb	2.204 lb
	500 gms	1lb $1\frac{2}{3}$ oz.	1 lb $1\frac{2}{3}$ oz
	100 gms	$3\frac{1}{2}$ oz	$3\frac{1}{2}$ oz
	10 gms	$\frac{1}{3}$ oz	$\frac{1}{3}$ oz
	453.59 gms	1 lb	1 lb
	226.80 gms	8 oz	8 oz
	28.35 gms	1 oz	1 oz
Volumes	1 litre	$1\frac{3}{4}$ pints	2 pints $1\frac{2}{5}$ fl. oz
	4.5 litres	1 gallon	1 gal. 1pint $\frac{3}{5}$ fl. oz
	3.79 litres	6 pints $13\frac{1}{2}$ fl. oz.	1 gallon
	568 mls	1 pint	1 pint $3\frac{1}{5}$ fl. oz
	473 mls	$16\frac{2}{3}$ fl. oz	1 pint
	28.4 mls	1 fl. oz	0.96 fl. oz
	29.6 mls	1.04 fl. oz	1 fl. oz

Some of the weight and volume conversions above have been approximated especially for use in the home, where the measurement of fractions of the ounce or fluid ounce is difficult.

Miscellaneous

1 Campden tablet in 4.5 litres (1 imperial gallon) = 50 ppm of sulphur dioxide, and is the same as adding 4.5 gms of Sodium metabisulphite to the same volume.

1 level 5 ml medicine spoon = approximately 5 grammes of sodium metabisulphite, enough to treat 25 litres with 100 ppm of sulphur dioxide.

TEMPERATURE
<u>CONVERSION CHART</u>

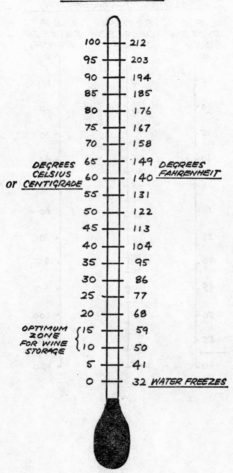

FIG. 26.

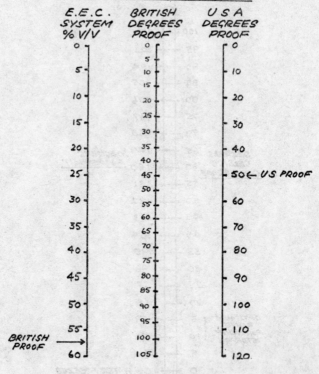

COMPARATIVE SCALES OF
ALCOHOLIC STRENGTH

Definitions

100° British Proof = 57.155% ethyl alcohol by volume at 20°C OR 57.1% v/v at 60°F.
100° U.S.A. Proof = 50.0% ethyl alcohol by volume at 60°F.

BIBLIOGRAPHY

Applied Wine Chemistry and Technology
A. Massel, published by Heidelberg Publishers Ltd., Southampton Row, London, W.C.1.

Chemistry and Technology of Wines and Liquors
Herstein and Jacobs, published by D. Van Nostrand Company Inc., New York, U.S.A.

Chemistry of Winemaking
A. Dinsmoor Webb, published by The American Chemical Society, Washington DC, U.S.A.

First Steps in Winemaking
C. J. Berry, published by The Amateur Winemaker Ltd., Andover, Hants.

Industrial Microbiology
Prescott and Dunn, published by McGraw-Hill Book Company Inc., New York, U.S.A.

Lehrbuch fur Weinbereitung und Kellerwirtschaft
W. Geiss, privately published by the Author, Bad Kreuznach, Rheinland, West Germany.

Scientific Winemaking—made easy
J. R. Mitchell, published by The Amateur Winemaker, Andover, Hants.

Technologie des Weines
Gerhard Troost, published by Verlag Eugen Ulmer, Stuttgart, West Germany.

The Bottlers Year Book
Published by B.Y.B. Limited, 7 Higher Drive, Purley, Surrey, CR2 2HP.

The Principles and Practice of Winemaking
W. V. Cruess, published by The AVI Publishing Co. Inc., New York, U.S.A.

The Science and Technique of Wine
L. Frumkin, published by H. C. Lea & Co. Ltd., London.

The Technology of Winemaking
Amerine and Berg, published by The AVI Publishing Company, Inc., Westport, Connecticut.

Winemaking and Brewing
Beech and Pollard, published by The Amateur Winemaker Ltd., Andover, Hants.

109

INDEX

INDEX